The Harvey House Cookbook

The Harvey House Cookbook

MEMORIES OF DINING ALONG THE SANTA FE RAILROAD

by
George H. Foster
and
Peter C. Weiglin

LONGSTREET PRESS
Atlanta, Georgia

Published by
LONGSTREET PRESS, INC.
A subsidiary of Cox Newspapers, Inc.
A subsidiary of Cox Enterprises
2140 Newmarket Parkway
Suite 118
Marietta, Georgia 30067

Printed in the United States of America

2nd printing 1999

Library of Congress Catalog Number: 91-77187

ISBN 1-56352-357-4

Cover and book design by Jill Dible
The text was set in Bembo by Laurie Shock Design
Cover photography by Al Clayton

Photo credits:
Special collections, University of Arizona Library – pgs. 7, 17, 27, 41, 81, 89, 105, 131, 143, 153, 165, 179

To Kurt Peter Cronheim, healer

and

To a Certain Lady from Cincinnati; had she lived in that time and been a Harvey Girl, the West would have been an even better place to live.

Contents

Preface

· ·

In this cookbook you will find two levels of "cooking experience," two levels of detail in the instructions. We have included recipes from two major time periods—from the column "In Harvey Service" in the Santa Fe Railroad magazine, circa 1910–13, and from the Fred Harvey employee magazine, *Hospitality*, published in the 1940s and 1950s. Readers will notice the difference in style, instructions, and use of ingredients between the two publications.

In a modern cookbook, recipes are precise, almost clinical, sometimes carried down to the level of grams and globules. But *The Harvey House Cookbook* is, by definition, not a modern cookbook, and we therefore assume that readers bring a certain level of understanding to the process. The older works, on which ours is modeled, often simply listed the ingredients for a sauce or garnish, for example, taking for granted that the chef knew what to do with them. We have, however, updated some references and names that have been lost in the mists of time.

We must acknowledge a little volume that was a most valuable translation tool from past to present names and ingredients. Entitled *A Selection of Dishes and the Chef's Reminder (A High Class Culinary Text Book)* (10th ed., 1909), a 220-page, gold-stamped vest pocket book bound in red leather, it was found, dust covered and forgotten, in the (long-closed) Harvey restaurant area of the Santa Fe station at Seligman, Arizona, a number of years ago. The book was a godsend, just as it must have been for chefs since its first publication in 1896. One example: an old Harvey recipe called for "Coxcomb," an item not widely known today. The old *Chef's Reminder* provided the answer; coxcomb (Fr. *crête du coq*) is the red comb of a rooster, crushed and used as a food coloring in the days before a rainbow of commercial colorings became available everywhere.

We are indebted to the great staff at the Kansas State Historical Society in Topeka, with special thanks to Connie Mennenger, curator of the Santa Fe Collection, and the staff of the photo section. Thanks also to Darrell D. Garwood, Cynthia Shively, and Margaret B. Knight, librarian.

We are grateful to Nedra Ross Moore, who shared the memories she has collected of former Harvey Girls in her native Kansas. Jere L. Krakow, historian by profession, who has a personal interest in Fred Harvey and is working on a comprehensive history of the Fred Harvey Organization, was kind enough to read the book in manuscript form. The help, counsel, and sharing of Ray Verr has been invaluable in the quest for Harvey collectibles. Thanks also to Mario Nick Klimiades, librarian and archivist of the Heard Museum; the Special Collections Department of the University of Arizona, Dr. Louis Hieb, department head, and Christine Leischow, library specialist; Margaret Bret-Harte, librarian, and her staff of the Arizona Historical Society; Michelle Gray of the Interlibrary Loan Department of the Tucson Public Library; and Michael A. Martin of the Santa Fe Railway. All of these good folks aided with the production of this volume.

The
Harvey House
Cookbook

CHAPTER ONE

In Search of a Decent Meal

· ·

No one individual did more to civilize the American West than Frederick Henry Harvey.

That plain and unequivocal statement might be easily dismissed in this era of hyperbole, where the word *greatest* is used too often by publicists to mean *barely adequate*. But Fred Harvey, founder of a hotel and restaurant chain that stretched from the Great Lakes to the Pacific Ocean, had a surprisingly strong social impact on the West and its history. This book hopes to recreate a bit of that history.

Before 1876, it was virtually impossible to get a decent American-style restaurant meal anywhere between the Mississippi River and the Pacific Ocean. Neither the ingredients for, nor the skill and equipment to produce, an outstanding meal were present in any quantity. Meat was in abundance—buffalo and antelope, for example—but it was quite likely tough. As for the aging of meat, an evening's dinner was quite likely to have been still walking or swimming around at noon.

Open flames, as those in campfires or pits, were the common heat source. Cast-iron kitchen ranges did not exist in America until the 1830s, and their weight and bulk made them prohibitively expensive to transport to the West. They were therefore exceedingly rare away from seaports until the railroads offered lower freight tariffs. Even so, the early stoves burned wood (later coal) and were incapable of maintaining constant temperatures.

Fruits and vegetables were only sporadically available, and what could be found was of questionable freshness, as refrigeration was unknown. Immersion in a cool stream or brook would help, but preservation involved salt and spices rather than cold temperatures. Baking of sourdough biscuits and similar items was done in portable tin Dutch ovens, as befit a basic cooking style derived from the pioneer caravan.

The most common early western dish appears to have been stew cooked in cast-iron kettles, with a wide and changing variety of ingredients from place to place and day to day, depending on what had been recently killed or was otherwise available. It is not difficult to divine how such synonyms for food as *chow*, *slop*, and *grub* entered the language.

This picture changed, however, as the expanding westward-moving railroads transformed the economics of transportation. Now, products that had not been available before the iron horse's arrival could be shipped more feasibly. In the late 1860s and early 1870s, railroads were built through the wild country between the Mississippi River and the advancing frontier. The first so-called transcontinental railroad line was, of course, the Union Pacific–Central Pacific route between Omaha and Sacramento, celebrated for its linkage at Promontory Point, Utah, in May 1869.

Even before the coming of the railroad, the Santa Fe Trail had been an artery of wagon-borne commerce. In the 1860s that old and well-worn path became the base for the Atchison, Topeka and Santa Fe Railway. Built west from Topeka, the first line segment of the new steel-rail technology opened in 1869. By late 1872 the Santa Fe had reached the Colorado border, and by 1878 it had stretched to Albuquerque, New Mexico.

In the next few years, Rock Island and Union Pacific rail lines also crossed Kansas between Kansas City and Denver, while the Chicago, Burlington and Quincy operated between Kansas City and Denver (via St. Joseph, Missouri) through Nebraska, immediately north of the Kansas border. Travelers thus had a choice of railroads to carry them westward.

Although the railroads reduced the time required for travel, eating during the trip was nothing less than a harrowing ordeal for the passengers. A train trip in that era was considerably different from what we came to expect in later years. For one, there were no dining cars. All trains had to stop to replenish the locomotive's water supply (at "tank towns") or to change engines about every hundred miles, so eating houses were built at some of these stops to feed the passengers at the same time. The railroads participated in this venture to the minimum possible extent; they were in the railroad business, not the food business. Most often, they leased trackside space to a local entrepreneur, who provided the food service in whatever ramshackle structure or tent he could provide. The average length of time for such stops was twenty minutes, which lent a sense of urgency to the gastronomic adventure awaiting the passenger.

American folklore is replete with travelers' tales of indigestible food (the grisly details of which have no place in a cookbook), hasty and indifferent service, and grayish "mystery meats" garnished with unidentifiable frying objects. They also faced exorbitant prices and the crowding, stampeding, and infighting caused by inadequate space in the railside establishments.

A traveling artist captured this scene of confusion in a railroad eating house as passengers scramble to finish their meals before the train departs. (Santa Fe Collections, Kansas State Historical Society)

Outrage was often added to frustration when the travelers had to pay in advance; the trains' departure times often came before any significant amount of food could be consumed. Indeed, suspicions arose that these loathsome eateries improved their profit pictures by "touching up" partially eaten meals left by hastily departing passengers and holding them for the subsequent delectation of the folks on the next train stopping there. Since no one had a chance to eat very much (and, in many cases, had no desire to do so), fatalities at least were rare.

Economists will tell you that this is the inevitable result of monopoly. When customers have no other choice, the tendency is toward high prices and poor quality of product and service. In this situation, the time, location, and duration of the meal stop were controlled by the railroad (for the convenience of the locomotives, remember); there was a lack of alternate facilities within range of the train; most

" For the business man who is in a hurry, the invalid who is in search of health, or the tourist who travels for pleasure, the GREAT MIDDLE ROUTE to the Pacific Coast has no equal in smoothness of track, elegance of equipment, diversity of scenery and interest, regularity of time, and certainty of connections."

◅ DIARY. ▻

First Day.—Leave Kansas City at 10.40 a. m.; Valley of the Kaw, 11.56 a. m.—Lawrence, the "historic city," and victim of the greatest tragedy of the late war; large dam and extensive manufactures; seat of Kansas State University. 1.15 p. m.—Topeka; home and original starting point of the Santa Fe Route; State capital; extensive yards and machine shops; population about 30,000; dinner. Afternoon—Fields, farms and orchards of Central Kansas; Osage coal-measures; civilization about fifteen years old. 3.50 p. m.—Emporia; population about 12,000; very wealthy in proportion to size; centre of richest agricultural and stock country in the United States; State Normal School. 5.15 p. m.—Florence; junction of line to El Dorado and rich southern counties. 6.45 p. m.—Newton; supper; heart of the now famous Cottonwood Valley, not long since an Indian-haunted wilderness, where even they and the buffaloes were considered badly off; junction of line to Wichita and southwestern counties of what is considered "old" Kansas.

Second Day.—7.40 a. m.—La Junta, Colorado; breakfast; junction, via Pueblo, for Denver, Colorado Springs, Manitou, Leadville, and the Gunnison country, Salt Lake City, Ogden, and all points in Northern Utah; have traversed during the night the great grazing region of Southwestern Kansas, and are now about 570 miles west of Kansas City. 12.25 p. m.—Pass through tunnel at Raton Pass and enter New Mexico. This is the ancient gateway of the "Santa Fe Trail," 7,622 feet high, and as nearly as it may be located, the crest of the continent. 1.35 p. m.—Raton; dinner; during the afternoon, pass through mountain scenery, Mexican settlements, coal-measures of New Mexico, and enter the wide, green meadows called "vegas." 7.30 p. m.—Town of Las Vegas; supper; train from here to Las Vegas Hot Springs; pleasure grounds, medicinal baths, cottages, and a good hotel—extensively visited by through and other travelers for baths, rest and mountain scenery.

DIARY.—Continued.

Third Day.—3.40 a. m.—Albuquerque; junction with Atlantic & Pacific line for all points in Southern California and for San Francisco direct; through Pullman cars placed in their proper places in trains for California, Old Mexico, and also to all points in Southern and Western Arizona and Southern California, via Deming and Benson, without disturbing passengers; during the night have passed Apache Canyon (daylight on return trip) and the Pueblo and Mexican settlements in the Rio Grande Valley. Lamy, junction for branch to old city of Santa Fe, was passed about midnight (stopping over at Las Vegas one train, it is reached at 1.40 p. m.) This little side-trip of seventeen miles is considered one of the most enjoyable in this country. 8.59 a. m.—Coolidge, N. M.—Here, during breakfast hour, baggage of through Pullman passengers is changed by porters from one car to corresponding sections in another, and the passenger makes the only change required of him without trouble, and often without knowing it. 1.54 p. m.—Holbrook; dinner. 8.00 p. m.—Williams; supper.

Fourth Day.—7.50 a. m.—The Needles; breakfast; crossing of Colorado River; during evening have passed (4.29 p. m.) that hideous crack in the face of the world called Canyon Diablo, and entered, about Flagstaff, the magnificent pine forest, through the shadows of which the train glides swiftly for nearly half the night. For the rest it has been that wide and treeless Arizona, across which is breaking the first dawn of civilization, a country of peaks and valleys, with wide pasture lands and occasional patches of sterility, and of which a vastness which makes the eyes ache is the prominent recollection. Here at The Needles begins, more or less interspersed with better country and diversified by mountain views which have no similitudes in any other region, the Desert—cacti, concrete, lava and silence—a picture as unique and long remembered as one where beauty is the only feature. 3.10 p. m.—Daggett; dinner. 6.00 p. m.—Mojave; supper; at Mojave the Southern Pacific Road takes up the Pullman coaches and places them at Oakland Pier at 10.40 the following morning. About twenty miles north of Mojave, and continuing for a distance of forty miles, are the wonderful scenes of Tehachapi Pass, probably unequaled on any other route in the world. Immediately east of Waterman is the junction with the California Southern, through cars direct to San Diego, via Colton, and to Los Angeles, San Bernardino, Riverside, Pasadena, Sierra Madre Villa, Santa Monica. This is the nearest and most direct line from the MISSOURI RIVER TO ALL POINTS IN SOUTHERN CALIFORNIA. These, very briefly, are a few of the features of the journey to the Pacific Coast by the Great Middle Route.

The diary of a typical four-day trip on the Santa Fe's California Limited between Kansas City and southern California, taken from an 1887 brochure published by the railroad. (Santa Fe Collections, Kansas State Historical Society)

passengers would never be seen at that stop again; and all of the western railroads had essentially the same level of "service." It is thus not surprising that railway dining was equated with misery—both during and after the meal.

One man changed those horrifying conditions. As we shall see, by providing good food and charming service across the region, a transplanted Englishman named Fred Harvey may well have done more than any other single person to civilize the American West. Out of the intersection of talent and opportunity would grow his famous Harvey Houses.

Dinner

· · · · · · · · · · · · · · · · ·

BLUE POINTS ON SHELL

FILETS OF WHITEFISH, MADIERA SAUCE

POTATOES FRANÇAISE

YOUNG CAPON, HOLLANDAISE SAUCE

ROAST SIRLOIN OF BEEF AU JUS   PORK WITH APPLESAUCE

TURKEY, STUFFED   CRANBERRY SAUCE

MASHED POTATOES   BOILED SWEET POTATOES   ELGIN SUGAR CORN

MARROWFAT PEAS   ASPARAGUS, CREAM SAUCE

SALMI OF DUCK   QUEEN OLIVES

BAKED VEAL PIE, ENGLISH STYLE

CHARLOTTE OF PEACHES, COGNAC SAUCE

PRAIRIE CHICKEN, CURRANT JELLY

SUGAR CURED HAM   PICKLED LAMB'S TONGUE

LOBSTER SALAD AU MAYONNAISE

BEETS

CELERY   FRENCH SLAW

APPLE PIE   COLD CUSTARD A LA CHANTILLY   MINCE PIE

ASSORTED CAKES   BANANAS   NEW YORK ICE CREAM

ORANGES   CATAWBA WINE JELLY   GRAPES

EDAM AND ROQUEFORT CHEESE

BENT'S WATER CRACKERS   FRENCH COFFEE

A sample Fred Harvey dinner menu from 1888. The price was 75 cents.

Appetizers

Canapé Danoise

Alfred Schaar, Chef, Dearborn Station, Chicago, Illinois

. . . .

White Bread
Anchovies
Eggs
Chives

Toast slices of white bread. Butter them. Cover each slice with filet of anchovies, chopped boiled eggs, and chives. Cut in triangles.

Cheese Straws

A. B. C. Dutcher, Manager of Topeka House, Kansas

. . . .

1 lb. flour
3/4 lb. grated cheese
Yolks of 4 eggs
Salt and pepper

Mix ingredients; salt and pepper to taste. Make into paste, roll out, cut in thin strips, and bake.

Relish Dish

Nelle Smith, Test Kitchen Supervisor

. . . .

Green onions
Radishes
Celery hearts
Rolls, corn bread sticks,
or muffins from any mix.

Arrange and serve.

Fruit Cup

Nelle Smith, Test Kitchen Supervisor

. . . .

Fresh pineapple
Sugar
Strawberries

Remove sharp leaf tips from the pineapple and, using pointed knife, cut around and remove crown. Then cut crosswise in $3/4$ inch slices. Cut off the rind and remove the "eyes." Cut crosswise and remove the core. Cut the pineapple into desired size, sprinkle with sugar (brown sugar gives an added taste), and place in covered dish in refrigerator for at least an hour. Remove hulls of fresh strawberries and place berries in colander; wash and drain thoroughly. Slice strawberries, saving enough whole berries to use as center *garni* for each fruit cup. Place berries in dish, sprinkle with sugar (determined by tartness of berry), cover, and chill before serving. Arrange fruit in chilled sherbet glasses, pouring some juice over fruit.

Guacamole Monterey

Joe Bianchi, Chef, El Tovar, Grand Canyon, Arizona

. . . .

1 avocado, mashed
1 tomato, chopped fine
1 tablespoon lemon juice
$1/2$ teaspoon chopped chives
$1/2$ teaspoon salt
Dash pepper
$1/2$ cup cottage or cream cheese
2 tablespoons chopped green onions
Dash Worcestershire sauce

Combine all ingredients thoroughly. Chill. Serve on lettuce with peeled, chilled tomato wedge or use as a dunk mixture. Yields $2 \, 2/3$ cups. Serves six.

DIPS

Nelle Smith, Test Kitchen Supervisor

. . . .

Note: Hundreds of dips could be listed. Room-temperature whipped cream cheese is a good base; bits of bacon, sardines, chili sauce, chopped fruits, and nuts may be added. Let your taste be your guide. Whip any cheese spread from the store, and add any of the following: pickle relish, diced ham, olives, green onions, or crumbled bacon. Use your own taste in seasonings, using catsup, horseradish, steak sauce, mustard, Tabasco, and Worcestershire. You'll find it easy to bring forth something different and very tasty.

Cheese Dip

. . . .

4 oz. crumbled bleu cheese

2 tablespoons milk

3 oz. softened cream cheese

2 tablespoons salad dressing

Combine ingredients in blender or beat well with electric mixer.

Onion Dip

. . . .

1 1/2 cup sour cream

2 oz. crumbled bleu cheese

2 tablespoons packaged onion soup mix

Mix onion soup mix and sour cream well. Stir in bleu cheese.

Cream Cheese and Olive Dip

Cream cheese
Chopped ripe olives
A-1 sauce

Mix all together.

Shrimp Dip

1 cup chopped shrimp
Milk
1 cup cottage cheese
$1/4$ cup chili sauce
$1/2$ teaspoon onion salt
1 tablespoon lemon juice
A-1 sauce to taste
Dash Tabasco sauce

Mix all ingredients except milk. Stir in enough milk to make good dipping consistency.

Easy Quickie Dip

3 oz. cream cheese, room temperature
1 $2^1/2$ oz. can deviled ham
1 tablespoon A-1 sauce

Mix all together.

Sauce for Shrimp

. . . .

3 tablespoons catsup

1 teaspoon lemon juice

3 tablespoons chili sauce

Dash Tabasco sauce

2 tablespoons horseradish

Combine all ingredients. Serve with shrimp.

Hot Mexican Bean Dip

. . . .

3 cups pork & beans in
tomato sauce

$^1/_2$ cup sharp cheese, shredded

1 teaspoon garlic salt

$^1/_2$ teaspoon salt

Dash red pepper

2 teaspoons vinegar

$^1/_2$ cup crisp bacon, chopped

1 teaspoon chili powder

2 teaspoons Worcestershire sauce

Combine all ingredients except bacon. Heat in chafing dish or in double boiler. Sprinkle chopped bacon over top.

CHAPTER TWO

Fred Harvey

· ·

When Frederick Henry Harvey stepped off the boat in New York City in 1850, the world took little notice. After all, he was a fifteen-year old lad from London, with approximately ten dollars—two pounds—in his pocket. That sum was not then as insignificant as it is today, but it was thin insulation against poverty.

In the Smith & McNeill Café, hard by the intersection of Washington and Barclay streets, one block from Pier 15 on the Hudson River, the young man found work as a dishwasher. The salary was two dollars a week. But the café was apparently a good one, and Frederick was intelligent and a willing worker and learner. There is no record of his having been involved with any eateries in London before his passage to America, nor is there any reason to suspect that such involvement in a British establishment would have contributed greatly to his culinary skills. For all practical purposes, therefore, we can regard New York as the place from which Fred Harvey embarked on a career that would change the face, and the digestion, of the American West.

The details of those early years in Fred Harvey's life are sketchy and subject to the self-serving (or company-serving) deletions and embellishments that often characterize the biographies of great individuals. It appears, however, that between one and two years after the beginning of his career in New York, Fred Harvey left for New Orleans, where he found work in a couple of restaurants. (It was later claimed by Fred Harvey's descendants that these establishments were among the finest in the Crescent City; regrettably, we have not been able confirm this claim.) If we assume that the character traits of hard work and stunning self-confidence for which he was later well known were already forming at that time, it is not too difficult to picture a young

The only known formal portrait of Fred Harvey.
(The Heard Museum Library)

man working his way up through sous-chef levels in kitchen hierarchies, even though he was not yet eighteen years of age.

The cumulative result was that Fred Harvey was exposed to, and learned from, good restaurant people in the two American cities where the culinary arts were most advanced in those days. Having seen and learned how it was done best, Fred now sought to transplant that knowledge to a new venue—St. Louis—then one of America's largest cities, thriving as the "Gateway to the West" even in those pre-railroad days. He moved there in 1853.

Becoming a U.S. citizen in 1858, Fred Harvey was headed for a prosperous business career. Within about a year, he realized his dream, to own and manage a prospering restaurant. He had also been active to some degree in a jewelry establishment and a clothing shop, but the restaurant seems to have been the primary goal, and his second love. The designation "first love" was reserved for Barbara Sarah "Sally" Mattas, who became Mrs. Fred Harvey in 1859.

Even though he had sold out his other interests to set it up, Fred was not the sole owner of this St. Louis restaurant, and the coming of the Civil War ruptured the partnership. Business declined in wartime, but that was not the killing blow. Harvey's sympathy lay with the North, and his partner's with the South. The telling day came in 1861, when Fred discovered that his partner had cleaned out the bank account and decamped to serve the Confederacy. The restaurant was shuttered, and Fred Harvey, virtually broke again, was looking for work.

After brief service on a Mississippi riverboat, Fred was hired as a mail clerk by the post office. In fact, Fred Harvey was one of the first two clerks hired for what became a revolutionary development in mail handling—the Railway Post Office, an operation featuring specially designed railcars in which mail was sorted while the train was rolling, with pickups and deliveries made in on-line towns along the way.

Exposure to the railroad business as a working passenger, based in St. Joseph, Missouri, opened Fred's eyes to the opportunities that the new industry provided. About 1863 he became a freight agent for a small railroad that later became part of the Burlington system. In 1865 he was promoted to general western agent, and transferred to Leavenworth, Kansas. The Harveys established residence there and made it their permanent home.

In addition to his railroad freight sales work, Fred also sold advertising for a newspaper; to say that he worked hard seems to be an understatement. There were other activities and investments as well. The Burlington was a heavy hauler of Texas cattle to midwestern and eastern markets, and Fred learned the cattle business. He even invested in a cattle ranch in 1867 and in a hotel in Ellsworth, Kansas, in 1868.

Since Fred Harvey's business activities had him riding the railroads much of the time, he was exposed to the truly abysmal food service then available on the railroads at that time. Not only would he join with the rest of the displeased rail travelers, but, given his experience and well-developed taste for good food, he would do something about it.

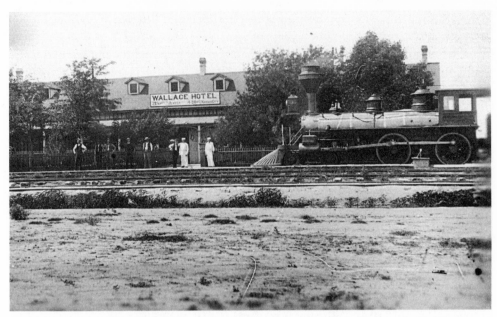

This hotel and eating house in Wallace, Kansas, was one of the three eating houses set up by Fred Harvey and Jeff Rice along the Kansas Pacific Railway, before Harvey's association with the Santa Fe. The locomotive is an "American Standard" type, which was used extensively before World War I.
(Santa Fe Collections, Kansas State Historical Society)

Between 1873 and 1875, Fred Harvey and a new partner, Jeff P. Rice, set up three railroad eating houses along the Kansas Pacific Railroad (later part of the Union Pacific). These were located along the railroad tracks at Lawrence and Wallace in Kansas, and in Hugo, Colorado. Operated more or less independently of each other, they are said to have prospered. We assume that the conditions in that trio of eating houses were a bit more sanitary and honest than average, but the partnership was dissolved by 1876. Jeff Rice apparently was less carried away by unprofitable notions involving quality and high standards.

By 1875, Fred Harvey was established as a prosperous salesman and manager, and along the way he had acquired considerable knowledge and experience in restaurant management and operation, railroad operations, cattle ranching, raising cattle for beef, hotel management, and advertising and promotion. Personally, he maintained an air of elegance and good taste, although he had also demonstrated that he could handle himself well in a fight. Further, Fred Harvey was a perfectionist in an imperfect world, easily irritated by matters that did not meet his standards. This combination of skills and irritants was poised at a moment in time to play a unique role in the development of the western United States. Fred Harvey had a spectacular solution to the western restaurant problem in mind. But had not a certain railway excursion trip gone awry, Harvey might not have been anything more than a successful Kansas businessman.

Soups

Albondigas Soup

Dan Tachet, Chef, Casteñeda, Las Vegas, New Mexico

. . . .

4 onions

1 lb. beef and veal, mixed

3 to 4 seeded green peppers

1 soupspoon of marjoram

2 cloves garlic

2 eggs

2 gallons of white bouillon

$^1/_2$ cup of corn meal

Parsley

Salt

Butter or lard

Cut up the onions and green peppers; put them on the fire in a copper pot with two ounces of lard or butter. (Mexicans do not use butter for cooking.) When onions are done or melted, add the bouillon and let boil. Have the beef and veal passed through a meat chopper. Add the eggs, marjoram, parsley, corn meal, and a little salt, and mix well. Make some small meat balls, about a half inch in diameter; drop them in the broth; let simmer for a half hour. Skim off the fat, season if necessary, and serve. (Mexican cooks will press the meat through their left hand over the simmering soup, using the forefinger of their right hand to give the albondigas the correct shape.)

Posole

. . . .

$^1/_2$ lb. lean pork, diced

1 tablespoon salad oil

2 cups hominy, drained

1 teaspoon salt

$^1/_8$ teaspoon pepper

Brown pork in hot oil; cover and simmer until tender. Add hominy seasoned with salt and pepper; cook 20 minutes. Serves four.

Cold Vichyssoise Cream

Charles Zuellig, Chef, Alvarado Hotel, Albuquerque, New Mexico

- -

4 medium potatoes,
peeled and sliced thin
$^1/_4$ cup onions, finely chopped
$^1/_2$ cup butter
2 quarts strained chicken stock
4 leeks
2 stalks celery, chopped fine
4 sprigs parsley
Salt and pepper
Dash of nutmeg
1 pint heavy sweet cream, scalded
2 bay leaves

Melt $^1/_2$ cup butter in a large kettle. Stir in four leeks, using only the white parts chopped very fine, and onions. Cook slowly until tender but not brown, stirring occasionally over a low heat. Stir in two quarts of hot strained chicken stock, four sprigs of parsley, celery, and potatoes. Season to taste with salt, pepper, a good dash of nutmeg, and two bay leaves. Cook until potatoes are tender. Rub the mixture through a fine sieve. Return to the fire, heat well, and stir in one pint heavy cream. Chill well before serving.

Corn Chowder Southern Style

- -

1 cup kernel corn
$^1/_2$ cup onions
$^1/_2$ cup celery
Bunch of soup greens
1 $^1/_2$ cups peeled tomatoes
$^1/_4$ lb. cubed salt pork
$^3/_4$ cup raw potatoes
4 cups chicken broth
$^1/_2$ cup sweet cream
1 teaspoon cornstarch
Spice bag of sage and thyme

Stew salt pork, corn, onions and celery, finely diced. Add chicken broth, diced raw potatoes and tomatoes, soup greens, and spice bag; let boil for one hour. Season with cayenne. Remove soup greens and spice bag. Finish by adding cream in which cornstarch has been dissolved.

Currant Soup

Fred Wendell, Inspector

. . . .

1 quart ripe currants
Cornstarch
Water

Run through a colander one quart of ripe currants that have been thoroughly washed, stemmed and carefully looked over. To one cupful of juice add half a cupful of water. Let it come to a boil. Sweeten just enough to take away the strong acid taste. Thicken with moistened cornstarch until the consistency of cream. Let it cook a few minutes to take away the raw cornstarch taste. Take from the fire, cool, and set away on ice. Serve very cold in sherbet glasses or bouillon cups.

Old-Fashioned Navy Bean Soup

Hans Mayr, Chef, The Bowl & Bottle, Chicago, Illinois

. . . .

1 cup navy beans
1 quart water
1/2 cup diced ham or ham bone
1 small clove garlic
1/4 teaspoon salt
1/2 cup butter
3 slices bacon, diced
1/2 cup chopped onion
1 tablespoon finely chopped leek
1/4 cup chopped carrot
1/3 cup chopped celery
2 tablespoons all-purpose flour
1 cup diced tomato
1 cup milk
1/4 teaspoon pepper

Wash beans and soak overnight in cold water to cover. Add ham, heat to boiling, cover and simmer three hours. Crush garlic with salt. Melt butter in a skillet and add garlic, salt, bacon, leek (if available), and onion; cook until onion is yellow and bacon is crisp. Add flour and cook two minutes, stirring constantly. Add to beans with remaining vegetables except tomato and cook 3/4 hour. Add tomatoes the last 15 minutes. Just before serving, add milk and pepper. Serves six.

Cream of Wisconsin Cheese Soup

Stanley S. Hamilton, Chef, St. Louis Union Station

. . . .

3 cups grated sharp Cheddar cheese
1 quart beef or chicken broth
3 tablespoons all-purpose flour
3 tablespoons butter or margarine
1 tablespoon Worcestershire sauce
1 cup light cream or top milk
$^1/_4$ teaspoon pepper

Melt cheese in two cups broth, stirring constantly. Add remaining broth; simmer until smooth. Melt butter, blend in flour, and add to first mixture with Worcestershire sauce and cream. Simmer 15 minutes, stirring constantly. Additional cream or milk may be added if desired. Season with salt, if needed, and pepper. Serve with hot toasted crackers. Serves six.

Note: Taste before seasoning, as cheese may make mixture salty enough.

CHAPTER THREE

The First Harvey Houses

· ·

What Fred Harvey had in mind in 1875 was nothing less than America's first interstate restaurant chain: a system of restaurants strung out along a railroad, operated in concert rather than independently, and providing a meal-stop food service that would attract, rather than repel, passengers. The railroad would serve as the direct delivery system for the fresh ingredients that would make up each day's bill of fare.

Fred first approached his railway employer, the Chicago, Burlington and Quincy. No interest. The second railroad he approached, early the following year, was the Atchison, Topeka and Santa Fe, and here the response was more positive, thanks to a failed excursion train involving celebrities.

The Santa Fe had installed some eating and dormitory facilities adjacent to, and often part of, passenger station facilities along its route. Its primary meal stop at Topeka had been started in 1874 under the management of a man identified as Peter Cline (or Kline). But, as in all the lines, the management believed that the railroad was not in the food business, and none of the western railroads yet saw what difference food could make in their operations.

Fred Harvey's visit couldn't have been better timed. The Santa Fe had just completed its rails to Pueblo, Colorado, in March 1876 and sought to celebrate, as railroads do, with an excursion train carrying a special guest list of distinguished passengers. This run had become a disaster, with inadequate food service and delays due to a blizzard, which made the lack of decent food even more harrowing. The result was an angry herd of half-starved railway executives, legislators, and other officials who were thrust into an unpleasant experience with "railroad food" that most of them had previously avoided. Food service was a very sensitive subject in the

Fred Harvey built his first dining operation for the Santa Fe in this wooden Topeka depot. Guests entered beneath the "Dining Hall" sign, shown at the far end of this 1880 photograph. For tired, hungry train travelers, the Irish Linen tablecloths, fine china, and delicious food were a surprising respite. Townspeople agreed that Fred Harvey's was the best restaurant in town. (The Heard Museum Library)

Santa Fe executive offices just as Fred Harvey walked into them.

Given the circumstances, Santa Fe Superintendent Charles Morse and President Thomas Nickerson were susceptible to Fred Harvey's idea. A significantly better food service would not only rehabilitate the Santa Fe's reputation but would also induce more passengers to choose the Santa Fe over the other railroads operating in the region. They decided that the state capital was the place to start; it would be most visible to the legislators, after all.

Negotiations between Fred Harvey, the Santa Fe, and Peter Cline resulted in closure of the Topeka lunchroom in the spring of 1876. The lunchroom premises were thoroughly cleaned and refurbished, English silver and Irish linen napery were purchased, and premium prices were paid for top-quality ingredients, condiments, and supplies. This time, although he hired Guy Potter to be the manager, Fred Harvey alone established the standards, and they were astonishingly above anything seen in Kansas up to that time. The lunchroom was kept spotless, the menu was unusually varied and of high quality, and the prices were moderate.

Success was instant and overwhelming. Railroad patrons were joined at counter and table by large numbers of railroad employees and local residents on a regular basis, something that had rarely if ever happened before at a railroad eating house. Skeptics wondered aloud and in print when the standards would go down, but they never did. People ate at the Harvey restaurant in Topeka even if they had the opportunity to choose another spot. It made the city a better place to live. In fact, one story claims that the Santa Fe management became concerned that Topeka was "clogging up" with people reluctant to leave the city and the Harvey food for westward points, and that they therefore asked Fred to open another restaurant down the line.

The railroad's "concern" sounds like an imaginative exaggeration, but a second location was placed under Harvey control early in 1878. This was a combination restaurant-hotel at Florence, Kansas, a division point one hundred miles west of Topeka. It should be noted that railroads customarily located division offices, crew-change points, and engine facilities approximately one hundred miles apart, with crews and locomotives assigned to a given division and operating between its boundaries or division points. Engines and crews on through trains would be changed at these division points. Then, as now, many railroad train-crew assignments involved traversing the division one way on a given day, to return home the following day. At the division-point locations, there were facilities for train crews to eat and to "lay over" one night. Railroads subsidized these meals and sleeping accommodations to varying degrees.

Clearly, the Santa Fe was aiming to provide facilities for both employees and passengers that were superior to those offered by any other railroad. It established a pattern that would endure through the years until the lineside eating houses were supplanted by dining cars, which happened gradually over the first half of this century. The Santa Fe Railroad owned the land and the buildings, and Fred Harvey operated the restaurant and hotel facilities, owning only those trappings attendant to his business. Railroad employees were issued meal tickets (called "pie cards") for free or discounted meals and accommodations.

The second "Harvey House," the Clifton Hotel in Florence, was upgraded from its previous mediocre status in the same way that the Topeka facility had been, with more English silver and Irish linen, and a chef was hired away from Chicago's elegant Palmer House hotel. That Harvey House chef was the highest-paid individual in Florence; nobody else came near his yearly $5,000 salary, not even the local bankers. The little town of Florence became famous for its Harvey House meals; the chef earned his money.

Meal prices at Harvey Houses in those days were usually a flat fifty cents in the dining room, slightly less at the lunch counter. That was a high price to pay, but fifty cents covered any meal on the menu, including a Kansas City steak, and the appetizers, portions, quality, and service were perceived as worth the price by virtually all of the customers.

Within about three years a third Harvey House was established. Guy Potter, Fred Harvey's first manager in Topeka, left in 1878 to set up a hotel-restaurant in Lakin, Kansas, two hundred miles west of Topeka. In 1881, the railroad bought the hotel in Lakin and moved the structure westward to Sargent (later known as Coolidge), Kansas, a distance of about fifty miles. At Sargent, Fred Harvey took over.

As Santa Fe main-line construction moved westward, new Harvey Houses opened up at the division/meal-stop points. By 1883, seven years after the Topeka

The facilities that became known as "Harvey Houses" were most often identified in the early days by signs that said, "Lunch Room" or "Eating House," with the subtitle "Fred Harvey, Mgr." The locals here are standing in front of the lunch room at Raton, New Mexico. (Special Collections, University of Arizona Library)

restaurant reopening, Fred Harvey was operating sixteen or seventeen Harvey Houses along the Santa Fe from Topeka, Kansas, to Albuquerque and Deming, New Mexico, some with hotels attached. In every place, townspeople found that the Harvey House had the best food in town. They joined the passengers and trainmen for meals at the depot.

In 1887, the Santa Fe reached California, through acquisition and extension of the Atlantic and Pacific Railroad. Fred Harvey's associate, David Benjamin, was dispatched to upgrade the horrifying beaneries on the A&P line under the Harvey House banner. When that job was done, the chain extended west of Albuquerque through Arizona to California.

The relationship that had started with a handshake on a town-by-town basis became more formal in 1889. In that year the railroad granted Fred Harvey the exclusive right to operate all of the railroad–owned eating houses and hotel facilities anywhere on the Santa Fe system west of the Missouri River.

The Harvey Houses made a profit despite their devotion to quality ingredients and furnishings and generous portions. The key to that profit was in what the railroad provided under the contract. Not only was there no rent paid to the railroad, but the railroad furnished free supplies, coal, water, ice, and transportation for Harvey House personnel.

The railroad's investment paid off. A large number of western railway passengers were intentionally choosing the Santa Fe Route for travel, citing the Fred Harvey food as the factor that made the difference in their choice. The Santa Fe was a clear winner in terms of market share.

It was now possible to get a decent meal in the American West.

Salads

Caesar Salad

. . . .

2 cups French bread croutons
6 tablespoons olive oil
Clove of garlic, split
2 heads romaine lettuce
1/4 teaspoon dry mustard
1/4 teaspoon black pepper
1/2 teaspoon salt
1/4 cup fresh lemon juice
5 anchovy filets, cut small
2 slightly beaten eggs
1/2 cup grated Parmesan cheese

Lightly brown croutons in small amount of olive oil flavored with split clove of garlic and set aside. Rub salad bowl with garlic, tear romaine into medium-sized pieces, place in bowl, and then add mustard, pepper, salt, cheese, olive oil, lemon juice, and anchovies; pour slightly beaten eggs over greens. Toss salad gently but thoroughly until no trace of egg is seen and all leaves are well coated. Just before serving, add croutons and toss lightly.

Chicken Salad

Frank Martin, Dining-car Chef

. . . .

Chicken
Celery
Hard-boiled Egg
Salt
Mayonnaise
Pepper
Oil
Vinegar
Capers
Heart of lettuce

Boil the chicken and cool in own liquid. Cut the breast into small dice. Take the white of celery, cut in dice and dry. Season with pepper, salt, oil, and vinegar, mixed well together. Serve in a bowl, with mayonnaise dressing on top and one hard-boiled egg cut in quarters, with capers and heart of lettuce in the center.

Potato Salad

Nelle Smith, Test Kitchen Supervisor

. . . .

1 quart potatoes, cooked and cubed

¹/4 cup celery, chopped

¹/4 cup onions, chopped

¹/4 cup green peppers, chopped

¹/4 cup half-and-half

¹/2 cup mayonnaise

2 hard-boiled eggs

2 tablespoons parsley, chopped

Salt to taste

White pepper to taste

Place potatoes, celery, onions, green peppers, parsley, and seasoning in mixing bowl. Mix together lightly; add half-and-half and mayonnaise; mix till vegetables are coated. (Note: Some potatoes absorb more dressing — you may have to add more mayonnaise.) Chop hard-boiled eggs and sprinkle over top of salad.

Tomato Salad

. . . .

Tomatoes, red and yellow

Onion juice

Lettuce

1 clove garlic

Watercress or parsley

French dressing

Tarragon vinegar

Select an equal portion of small red and yellow tomatoes. Lightly scald the tomatoes, peel carefully at once and set away to chill. At serving time, rub the salad bowl or small platter with a cut clove of garlic and line it with heart leaves of lettuce. Put the yellow tomatoes in the center and the red ones around them. At the sides and ends put a compact little bunch of dark green cress or parsley. Pour carefully over the tomatoes a highly seasoned French dressing flavored with tarragon vinegar and a few drops of onion juice.

German Potato Salad

. . . .

12 potatoes

Finely sliced onions

1 teaspoon salt

1/2 teaspoon pepper

1 egg yolk

3 tablespoons olive oil

Chopped parsley

4 tablespoons vinegar

1/2 cup boiling water or broth

Boil twelve potatoes. While hot cut in thin slices, cover with finely sliced onions and add one teaspoonful of salt and one-half teaspoonful of pepper. Mix the yolk of one egg with three tablespoonfuls of olive oil and four tablespoonfuls of vinegar. Pour the well-mixed dressing over the potatoes, then pour a half cupful of boiling water or broth over the whole mixture and stir well. Sprinkle with chopped parsley; cover and let stand a few hours. This salad will never be dry.

New England Scallop Salad

Ernest A. Spinuler, Chef, Victor Hugo Inn, Laguna Beach, California

. . . .

2 lbs. sea scallops, cooked

1 cup diced celery

1 cup diced cucumbers

1/4 cup sliced ripe olives

1 cup sliced cooked mushrooms

Lettuce leaves

1 cup French dressing

1 tablespoon diced pimentos

Salt and pepper

Lemon juice to taste

Cut scallops into bite size pieces; combine with celery, cucumbers, mushrooms, olives, and pimentos. Add French dressing; chill for two hours. Add salt, pepper, and lemon juice to taste. Serve on lettuce leaves in scallop shells or salad plates. Serves six. Optional: garnish to your liking with tomato wedges, asparagus spears, or carrot curls.

Poinsettia Salad

Nelle Smith, Test Kitchen Supervisor

. . . .

Grapefruit
Salad greens
Orange peel or
Grated American cheese

Eight segments of grapefruit (use pink or color the plain with red food coloring). Arrange the grapefruit to resemble the poinsettia blossom, on any fresh greens. Grate some orange peel or American cheese in the center.

Caruso Salad

Charles Zuellig, Chef, Alvarado Hotel, Albuquerque, New Mexico

. . . .

Lettuce
Tomatoes
Pineapple

Mix and top with French dressing.

Salad

Nelle Smith, Test Kitchen Supervisor

. . . .

Avocado pear
Tomato
Lettuce

Choose an avocado that is soft. Avocados should be a rich green with no brown spots. Cut the avocado in half, remove seed, pare, and cut in wedges and place on lettuce. Garnish with tomato wedges.

Maurice Salad

. . . .

1/2 cup breast of turkey julienne

1/2 cup baked ham julienne

1 tablespoon pickle relish

Hearts of 2 heads of lettuce

1/3 cup tomatoes julienne

4 tablespoons mayonnaise

3 tablespoons olive oil

1 teaspoon chopped chives

2 tablespoons distilled cider vinegar

1 teaspoon Worcestershire sauce

Hard-boiled eggs

Tomato wedges

Toss together turkey, ham, pickle relish, lettuce, and julienne tomatoes. Blend ingredients for dressing thoroughly, pour over greens, and lightly toss. Place salad on chilled plates and garnish each with chopped chives, chopped hard-boiled egg, and tomato wedges.

Tossed Greens with Apples

Nelle Smith, Test Kitchen Supervisor

. . . .

3 quarts washed and torn greens

1/2 cup green onions, chopped

2 cups sliced apples,

washed and cored

Salt and pepper to taste

Place greens, onions, and apples in large bowl; toss lightly. Add enough dressing to coat greens; sprinkle cheese and pepper over top. Serves six.

Roman Dressing

Stanley Hamilton, Chef, St. Louis Union Station, Missouri

. . . .

2 1/2 garlic cloves, chopped
1 1/2 teaspoons salt
1 cup salad oil
1 egg, well beaten
Juice of 1 lemon
1/3 cup grated Parmesan cheese
2 teaspoons whole
peppercorns, ground
3/4 tablespoon Worcestershire sauce

Mash garlic with salt. Add oil slowly to beaten egg, beating constantly with rotary or electric beater. When mixture starts to thicken, add oil and lemon juice alternately in small amounts, beating constantly. Stir in cheese, ground pepper, Worcestershire sauce, and garlic salt. Yields about 1 2/3 cups.

French Dressing

A. B. C. Dutcher, Manager, Harvey House, Topeka, Kansas

. . . .

One part tarragon vinegar
Four parts olive oil
Paprika
Salt and pepper

Mix very thoroughly, having a piece of ice in the bowl. (Note: Although Fred Harvey would not sanction the use of anything but olive oil of the very highest grade, those to whom the flavor of olive oil is distasteful will find peanut oil an excellent substitute. It is much less expensive and cuts the vinegar equally as well, producing a most palatable dressing.)

Chiffonade Dressing

Alfred Schaar, Chef, Chicago Dearborn Station, Illinois

. . . .

Parsley
Red beets
Eggs
French dressing

Finely chop equal parts of parsley, red beets, and hard-boiled eggs, and mix with French dressing.

Lemon Dressing

Nelle Smith, Test Kitchen Supervisor

. . . .

Sour cream
Lemon juice
Salt and pepper

To prepare, stir lemon juice into sour cream, and add salt and pepper (amount of lemon juice according to tartness desired).

Dressing for Fruit Salad

Nelle Smith, Test Kitchen Supervisor

. . . .

1 cup sour cream
2 tablespoons honey
Juice from maraschino cherries
1 tablespoon lemon juice

Whip together sour cream, honey, and lemon juice. Add enough cherry juice to give a pink color.

Fruit Salad Cream Dressing

Nelle Smith, Test Kitchen Supervisor

. . . .

1 cup sour cream
1/4 cup honey

Stir together. Pour over salad ingredients until all are coated.

CHAPTER FOUR

The Harvey System

. . . .

Fred Harvey demanded, firmly and with no exceptions, that every employee maintain the highest food-preparation and service standards, at all times, in every location. That insistence can scarcely be overstated.

The same high standards applied to hotels, where accommodations received as close attention to detail and quality as in the restaurants. Wherever one went, a passenger could be sure of a room with a real bed, clean and uninhabited by other than the human occupant. And this at rates that otherwise were being charged for little more than a horse stall.

Operating procedures in the Harvey House restaurants were worked out in great detail; there was a rigidly defined way to do everything that needed doing: quantities, measurements, procedures, times, and results. The impression on a traveling customer, therefore, was of a consistent high quality, regardless of which Harvey House was being visited. An additional benefit was that any Harvey-trained person could move from Harvey House A to Harvey House B and immediately begin operating at close to peak efficiency.

The peculiarities of train feeding made efficiency mandatory. Each Harvey House might be scheduled to serve from two to six train meal stops during the course of a day. Conductors and trainmen would ask passengers about meal preferences while the train was en route. Legend has it that a series of whistle signals conveyed the information to the Harvey House up ahead, but it is more plausible that the information about numbers of passengers and desires was dropped off at a telegraph station (whether the train stopped or not) and wired ahead to the restaurant. The whistle signal was merely a standard way to alert the restaurant that the train was about a mile away. Even forearmed with some idea of what was to be expected of them, the Harvey House staff had only about twenty to thirty minutes to feed sixty to one hundred people. That they were able to accomplish this without the passengers feeling rushed was a tribute to their training and organization.

Beverage preparation, for example, clearly shows how service was streamlined to maximize customer satisfaction during a limited meal stop. As a customer was seated, his or her beverage preference was determined. Then, if necessary, the Harvey Girl who inquired adjusted the cup at the customer's place setting. A few minutes later one or two other Harvey Girls came down the line with pitchers and, without any further instructions, distributed coffee, tea, or milk to the appropriate patrons.

To some patrons the process seemed to border on the occult, but the key was a systemwide cup code. The code was subject to some minor variations over time since its development during the 1880s, but these were the basics, found at any and all Harvey Houses:

Cup upright in the saucer: coffee
Cup upside down in the saucer: hot tea
Cup upside down, tilted against the saucer: iced tea
Cup upside down, away from the saucer: milk

Of course, sometimes customers found themselves with a beverage other than that which they had ordered. Upon complaining, they would find that the difference occurred because the customer had fiddled with the cup. Adjustments were swiftly and cheerfully made, of course.

One Fred Harvey requirement was that gentlemen wear jackets in the dining room. For those who forgot, a few spare jackets were kept on hand at the entrance. One patron in Oklahoma sued over this requirement; the state supreme court decided in Fred Harvey's favor on appeal.

The whole process was monitored closely by the Harvey company's headquarters to ensure that the standards were not being violated. The first headquarters office established by Fred Harvey was in his town of residence, Leavenworth, Kansas. (Curiously, there is no record of a Harvey House in Leavenworth, even though it was at the end of a Santa Fe branch line.) It was in a Leavenworth bank that Fred had found David Benjamin, its cashier, to be an outstanding analyst of reports. Benjamin became a steady provider of financial and statistical advice, and in 1881 he became Fred Harvey's general manager and second-in-command. Benjamin moved his offices, and consequently the Fred Harvey company headquarters, from Leavenworth to a small office in the Kansas City Depot, on the Santa Fe's main line.

Daily reports to Headquarters were filed from each location, covering every detail of the operation. These reports were scrutinized to flag possible problems. For example, a report of a lower-than-average per-portion food cost was more likely to cause suspicion than jubilation. More than one new manager was dismayed to find himself reprimanded or fired for getting more portions out of a given quantity of raw

In the 1890s, the Santa Fe railroad repainted some buildings and gave itself featured billing on dining room signs, as was done here in Kingman, Arizona. In this photo, taken about 1905, townspeople and passengers watch as two locomotives bring a train into town. (Library of Congress)

materials. After all, he was just following standard industry practices. Those were decidedly not Fred Harvey's standards.

In addition to purchases by Headquarters, local Harvey House managers had the authority, indeed the duty, to keep track of local food producers and to purchase local eggs, poultry (including quail), vegetables, and other items if they were of high enough quality. Those purchases were most often made in large quantity, enough to be used in part or all of the Harvey system.

The railroad's telegraph wires furnished the communications that allowed Headquarters to coordinate the whole effort. A small fleet of express refrigerator cars assigned to "Harvey House Restaurant Supply" shuttled back and forth with ingredients and supplies gathered from all over, bringing, for example, quality meat westward from Kansas City slaughterhouses and fresh fruit and vegetables eastward from California farms. Those refrigerator cars provided each restaurant with an unequaled warehouse and delivery system.

The daily menus for breakfast, lunch, and dinner were supplied and tightly controlled by Headquarters, and they varied from day to day. Menus were sent to the restaurants in four-day cycles. The aim was to ensure that a traveler on the Santa Fe would not see the same choices a second time during his or her trip on the railroad. The menus were based on what foods were available and in season, and coordinated

The "Lunch Room" signs remained as the towns grew, with larger brick stations replacing the original wood structures. Here, in Emporia, Kansas, the bustle of train time circa 1910 takes place in front of the lunch room in which noted editor William Allen White savored Fred Harvey food. White's nationally syndicated writings contributed to the national prominence of Fred Harvey and the Santa Fe. (Special Collections, University of Arizona Library)

with the eastbound and westbound manifests for the express refrigerator cars that carried ingredients and supplies back and forth along the line.

The significance of Fred Harvey's "express" refrigerator cars assigned to Dining Room Supply service was that they were part of scheduled passenger trains, not the slower and less certain freight trains on the railroad. Thus, while passenger trains were stopped for water and meals, one or two of the Harvey House employees would unload and load supplies, as called for by the menu or local purchases.

Sometimes the law determined part of the menu. In the state of Kansas, for example, a law passed in 1900 forbade serving game birds at restaurants. The Harvey system had to accommodate this restriction, although the birds may have been raised on a Harvey ranch and were perfectly legal in other states. In similar fashion, local liquor laws were different from place to place. Even on moving trains, passage through "dry" territory meant closing up the liquor cabinet for the duration.

"The Boss" and his two primary assistants, David Benjamin and Byron Schermerhorn, spent a great deal of time away from Leavenworth, monitoring operations. Fred Harvey perfected the Sudden Unannounced Visit as a quality-control device. In its most disconcerting form, Fred Harvey would suddenly loom in the doorway of a given Harvey House and proceed to conduct an inspection that would have pleased the most stringent Prussian *Obersleutnant*. Uniforms, fingernails, dishes and place settings, food lockers, and other facilities all came under the sharpest scrutiny. There was even a white-glove or handkerchief inspection of nooks, crannies, door lintels, and picture frames.

Failure to measure up did not result in a report being filed and preparation of a fifteen-page plan for corrective action within the next six months. Action came a great deal sooner and more decisively. In more than one case, Fred Harvey literally tossed the offending manager out onto the station platform to emphasize the immediate termination of employment. The Boss's dissatisfaction with the accuracy of a table setting was often shown by grabbing the tablecloth and spraying china, English silver, and Irish linen all over the floor. This maneuver was accompanied by a gruff order to "fix it right this time."

Gradually, a corps of managers and staff who understood the unremitting need for customer satisfaction was assembled and trained to Fred Harvey's methods and definition of what was acceptable. But in the first years, too many of the male employees were either unreliable or footloose, or became injured in fights and unavailable for work. It was a hazard of living for all men in pioneer western towns. A solution to that problem, and a number of others, was soon to come.

Fred Harvey maintained two dairies in the system; the first and largest was at Las Vegas, New Mexico, where milk was produced and bottled for Harvey Houses and Santa Fe dining cars. This milk bottle cap survives from a later era and illustrates Fred Harvey private label markings.

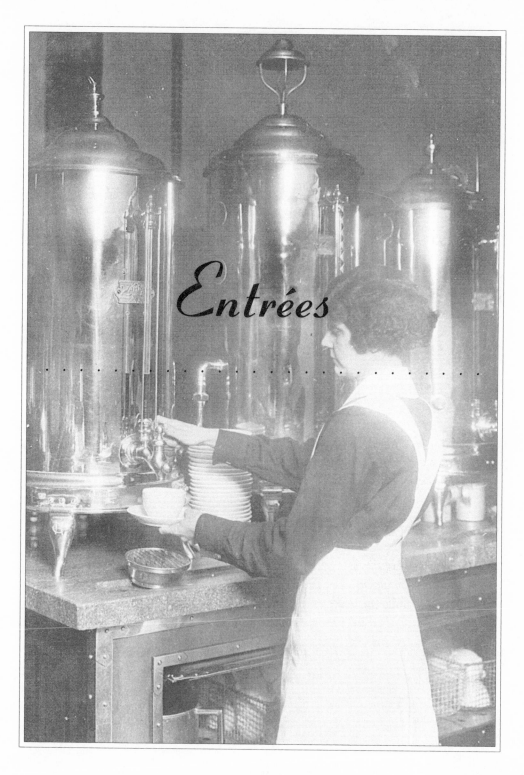

Entrées

Many of the sauces used in the entrée recipes can be found
in the Sauces chapter later in this book.

. . . .

Tournedos of Beef, Marco Polo

Lewis Eklich, Chef, Cleveland Union Terminal Restaurants, Ohio

. . . .

8 6-oz. beef tenderloins

Sauté beef tenderloins. Place wild rice on a dinner plate; then place beef tenderloin on the bed of wild rice, cover tenderloin lightly with Marco Polo sauce and top generously with garnish. Sprinkle chopped parsley on top. Serves eight.

1 ^{1}/$_2$ cups wild rice, washed
and drained
^{1}/$_2$ cup minced onion
1 tablespoon bacon fat
1 ^{1}/$_2$ cups beef stock

Wild Rice

Mix together and bake in oven for 40 minutes at 375 degrees.

5 oz. bamboo shoots
5 oz. bean sprouts
5 oz. sliced water chestnuts
^{1}/$_2$ cup mushrooms
2 oz. butter

Garnish

Mix together and sauté in the butter.

Beef Stroganoff

Frank DeBerry, Chef, Old Spinning Wheel Restaurant, Hinsdale, Illinois

. . . .

2 lbs. filet of beef, thin strips
1 tablespoon flour
2 tablespoons tomato juice or paste
2 cups beef stock
3 tablespoons heavy sour cream
5 tablespoons butter
3 tablespoons grated onion
or chopped shallot

Sprinkle strips of beef generously with salt and pepper and let stand for two hours in a cool place or in refrigerator. Blend flour with three tablespoons butter in saucepan over low heat until a roux forms, bubbles, and is smooth. Gradually stir in beef stock and cook mixture until it begins to thicken. Boil for two minutes and strain through fine sieve into large saucepan. Add heavy sour cream alternately with tomato juice or paste, stirring constantly. Simmer sauce gently. Do not boil. Sauté beef in skillet in three tablespoons butter with grated onion or chopped shallot. Add contents of skillet to sauce; taste for seasoning. Simmer meat gently without boiling for 20 minutes. Serve with rice pilaf or potato balls, as well as thin slices of dark bread generously buttered.

Minute Steak Au Chambertin

Roy Miller, Chef, Kansas City Union Station, Missouri

. . . .

6 10-oz. minute sirloin steaks
Salt and pepper to taste
Butter as needed
7 shallots finely chopped
6 oz. Chambertin wine
1 cup rich brown sauce
1 cup 25 percent cream

Season well-trimmed steaks, sauté in butter, and arrange on platter. Sauté shallots to a golden brown in same pan, add wine, and reduce to a minimum. Stir in brown sauce, whipping constantly until mixture comes to a boil. Add cream and remove. Pour over steaks. Serves six.

Flank Steak

Ed Plowman

. . . .

Flank steak

2 oz. beef marrow

Garlic

4 or 5 green onions

Flour

Butter

1 cup consommé

Parsley

Salt and pepper

Worcestershire sauce

Toast

Cut up four or five green onions with one or two ounces of beef marrow or a little fat surrounding the beef kidney. If the steak is too thick, split it in two with a sharp knife, and make a slight incision crosswise on each piece. Season with salt and pepper, rub with a bruised clove of garlic, cut the steak in four or five pieces, roll in flour, and fry in clarified butter. When done, remove the steak into another pan, cover with the green onions and marrow, and set in oven. Throw a pinch of flour into the pan where the steak was cooked, let it get slightly brown, add a cup of consommé, stir and let cook for a few minutes. Add to the gravy a little parsley, a piece of butter, and a tablespoonful of Worcestershire sauce, but do not boil. Pour onto a platter and put the steak in, with onions on top. Serve with toast as a garnish.

Filet Mignon de Chef

Tage Eriksen, Chef, Kungsholm Restaurant, Chicago, Illinois

. . . .

4 filets mignons
1 1/2 cups sour cream
1/2 tablespoon chopped parsley
1/2 cup brandy
1 1/2 teaspoons butter
Salt
1/2 cup demi-glace sauce
or beef consommé
Freshly ground pepper to taste

Sauté filets medium rare in butter. Pour brandy over the filets and flame. Remove from pan and keep warm. Add demi-glace or consommé to drippings in pan. Salt and pepper to taste and cook over low flame. Stir in sour cream and parsley. (Don't let the sauce boil or it will separate.) The meat can be served with Lyonnaise potatoes and the sauce served on the side. Serves four.

Tenderloin Tips of Beef Picante

Eli Gomez, Chef, Bright Angel Lodge, Grand Canyon, Arizona

. . . .

1 1/2 lbs. beef tenderloin
(cut into 1/2 inch-thick strips)
1 teaspoon salt
1/4 cup shortening
1 small clove garlic
(crushed in a little salt)
1 onion, diced
1/3 cup flour
1 medium bell pepper, diced
1 medium pimento, diced
1/8 teaspoon ground bay leaf
1/8 teaspoon ground cloves
1 quart beef broth
1 cup red chili powder
1/3 cup sherry wine

Season meat with salt and sauté in shortening to a light brown. Add garlic and onion and sauté a little longer. Stir in flour and blend well. Add all remaining ingredients and cook until tender. Serve with pearl onions and new peas in a casserole.

Plantation Beef Stew on Hot Biscuits

John Darden, St. Louis Union Station, Missouri

. . . .

1 1/2 lbs. beef cut into
1 1/2 inch cubes
1 quart hot water
1/2 cup diced onion
2 cups diced potatoes
1 clove garlic, minced
6 green onions, chopped
6 three-inch biscuits
1 1/2 teaspoon salt
1/4 teaspoon coarsely and freshly
ground black pepper

Cover meat with water; cover and simmer for 1 1/2 hours. Add one cup diced potatoes; cook for one hour until potatoes become mushy. Add remaining vegetables and seasonings; cook until vegetables are just tender (20 to 25 minutes). Serve over split hot biscuits. Serves six. Variations of this stew may be made by using chicken, veal, pork, or ham in place of beef.

Beef Steak Frascati

Finn Sorensen, Chef, Kungsholm, Chicago, Illinois

. . . .

4 12-oz. beef tenderloins
(meat flattened as thin as possible)
4 egg yolks
1 teaspoon capers
Several sprigs of chopped parsley
Garlic salt
4 teaspoons chopped onion
Bordelaise Sauce

Spread egg yolk on each tenderloin, then sprinkle them with capers, onions, parsley, and garlic salt. Fold meat over. Take a knife and press edges of meat together to seal. Heat butter in frying pan and brown meat about two or three minutes on each side. Serve with Bordelaise Sauce.

Roulade of Beef

Erich Walther, Santa Fe, New Mexico

· ·

4 8-oz. pieces sirloin butt
2 teaspoons salt
¹/₄ teaspoon pepper
4 slices bacon
2 thick slices onion, cut in half
1 large dill pickle,
cut lengthwise into fourths
¹/₄ cup all-purpose flour
4 teaspoons butter
1 tablespoon all-purpose flour
2 cups beef broth
2 tablespoons catsup

Flatten steaks with meat cleaver until very thin; season with salt and pepper. On each steak, place a slice of bacon, ¹/₂ onion slice, and one pickle stick. Roll up steak and tie with string. Roll in ¹/₄ cup flour and saute in butter until well browned. Add 1 tablespoon flour to butter. Add broth and catsup, cover pan and cook slowly for 30 minutes. Remove string before serving. Serves four.

Bright Angel Mexican Salisbury Steak

Eli Gomez, Chef , Bright Angel Lodge, Grand Canyon, Arizona

· ·

2 ¹/₂ pounds lean ground beef
2 ¹/₂ ounces pimento, diced
8 oz. green chili pepper, diced
1 large onion, diced fine
6 oz. bread crumbs
2 eggs beaten lightly
Salt and pepper
Red Chili Sauce

Combine all ingredients except red chili sauce. Shape into six patties. Broil or grill the patties to desired "doneness." Serve with Red Chili Sauce. Serves six.

Ground Beef in Sour Cream Sauce

Nelle Smith, Test Kitchen Supervisor

. . . .

1 cup chopped onion

3 cups tomato juice

2 tablespoons fat

1 teaspoon salt

1 lb. ground beef

1 1/2 teaspoons celery salt

3 cups medium noodles

Dash pepper

2 teaspoons Worcestershire sauce

1 cup dairy sour cream

1/4 to 1/2 chopped green pepper

Green pepper rings

1 3-oz. can (2/3 cup) sliced
mushrooms, drained and sautéed

Cook onion in hot fat until tender but not brown. Add beef; brown lightly. Place noodles in layer over meat. Combine tomato juice and seasonings; pour over noodles. Bring to boiling; cover and simmer over low heat 20 minutes. Add green pepper; cover and continue cooking 10 minutes or till noodles are tender. Stir in sour cream and mushrooms; heat just to boiling. Season to taste. Top with green pepper rings. Serves six.

Beef Rissoles

George Burnickel, Chef, California Limited

. . . .

Cold cooked beef, minced, three parts

Grated bread crumbs, one part

Egg yolks

Lemon Rind

Mashed potatoes

Roast beef gravy

Salt and pepper

Herbs

Mix and season beef with herbs, grated rind of lemon, salt, and pepper. Bind with raw yolks of eggs, make into the shape of an egg, bread, and fry. Serve with a mound of mashed potatoes in the center of the dish, a rissole at each end and side, and thickened roast beef gravy poured around. Garnish potatoes with parsley. This dish may be served also with kidney beans, green peas, French-cut string beans, or mixed vegetables instead of the potatoes. Serves six.

Scallopini of Veal, Marsala

Louis Sagno, Chef, Los Angeles Union Station, California

2 lbs. veal steak, cut in 1 $^1/_2$ inch pieces

1 small onion, finely chopped

1 clove garlic, minced

2 tablespoons all-purpose flour

2 tablespoons butter

2 teaspoons salt

$^1/_4$ teaspoon pepper

$^1/_2$ cup Marsala or sherry wine

$^1/_2$ lb. fresh mushrooms, sliced

Brown veal, onion, and garlic in butter. Sprinkle with flour, salt, and pepper. Add wine, cover, and simmer about 15 minutes. Add mushrooms and continue cooking about seven minutes. Makes four large servings. (This dish is excellent served with Risotto.)

Breaded Veal Cutlet Zingara

George Lee Barker, Chef, *Super Chief*

4 veal cutlets, pounded thin

2 tablespoons chopped tongue

2 tablespoons chopped hard-boiled egg

1 cup tomato sauce

$^1/_2$ cup grated Swiss cheese

2 tablespoons chopped ripe olives

2 eggs

1 cup milk

Salt and pepper

Bread crumbs

1 cup flour

Make egg wash of eggs and milk. Dip veal cutlets in flour, egg wash, and bread crumbs. Sauté until brown on both sides. In casserole put tomato sauce with chopped ham, tongue, egg, and olives. Arrange browned cutlets on sauce. Sprinkle with grated cheese. Brown under broiler.

Veal Piccata

Max Wuthrich, Chef, The Music Center, Los Angeles, California

2 lbs. veal short loin

Zucchini

Salt

Flour

Eggs

Butter or oil

Ground white pepper

MSG

Lemon juice

Chopped parsley

Brown gravy

4 oz. tomatoes

Button mushrooms

Artichoke bottoms

Purée of green peas

Slice two pounds of boneless, skinless, and fatless veal short loin into 24 pieces and pound into scallopini with a mallet. Cut 24 slices of zucchini $1/8$ inch thick and same overall size as the scallopini. Season zucchini with salt, dip in flour, then in lightly beaten eggs and pan fry in clarified butter or coconut oil until golden brown. Set aside and keep warm. Season veal scallopini with mixture of salt, ground white pepper, and monosodium glutamate. Dip in flour, then in lightly beaten eggs and pan fry on both sides until golden brown. In the center of a large oval platter, alternate each scallopini with a slice of zucchini in two rows from end to end. Sprinkle with fresh lemon juice and chopped fresh parsley. Surround the meat with a cordon of good thin brown gravy. Melt four ounces whole butter in a skillet and bring to a hazelnut color before pouring over veal and zucchini. Surround the Piccata with four ounce tomatoes hollowed out and filled with sautéed button mushrooms and 2 $1/4$ inches in diameter boiled artichoke bottoms sauted in butter and stuffed with a purée of green peas. Serves eight. For color contrast, alternate each tomato with an artichoke bottom. (Note: Artichoke bottoms are available commercially, frozen or canned in brine.)

Veal Bourguignonne

Nicholas Bauernhuber, Chef, Albuquerque Airport, New Mexico

. . . .

1 veal ribeye, 4–5 lbs.

12 oz. bacon fat

Salt and black pepper to taste

2 garlic cloves

1 medium-sized chopped onion

2 bay leaves

Pinch of sweet basil

$^1/_2$ gallon beef stock

1 cup Burgundy wine

Juice of 1 lemon

2 lbs. small whole potatoes

4 oz. tomato purée

1 lb. mushrooms

2 lbs. pearl onions

Place veal in deep roasting pan and add chopped garlic cloves, salt, and coarse black pepper and rub the meat with bacon fat. Brown both sides of meat quickly then add chopped onions, bay leaves, sweet basil, beef stock, and tomato purée. Cover the meat and simmer for 40 to 50 minutes. Add $^1/_2$ cup of Burgundy wine. Remove meat from mixture and roast in a medium oven until well browned. Slice meat (two slices per portion) and keep hot. Add the second half cup of Burgundy wine and lemon juice to liquid, strain, and reduce it to about a pint. Garnish the meat with small glazed onions, sautéed mushroom caps, and Parisienne browned potatoes. Pour wine sauce over meat slices and serve.

Pork Chops

John Frye, Chef, Ranch House and Club Houses, Valencia, California

6 pork chops
6 potatoes
3 onions
1 cup chicken stock
Accent
Flour
Oregano
Salt and pepper

Flour pork chops and grill lightly on both sides. Arrange on bottom of roasting pan. Season with salt, pepper, Accent, and oregano. Sauté onions and spread over chops. Cover with a layer of sliced raw potatoes. Add chicken stock. Cover and seal with foil. Baking time: approximately 1 $1/2$ hours in a 350-degree oven.

Pork Chops Bavarian

John Frenden, Chef, Chicago Union Station

6 thick pork chops
1 $1/2$ lbs. raw sauerkraut
1 lb. can tomatoes
1 medium-sized onion
1 clove garlic
1 whole bay leaf
1 teaspoon sugar
Salt and pepper to taste
6 raw tomatoes, sliced thick
Potatoes

Brown pork chops in skillet, remove, and put in sauerkraut, onion diced fine, clove of garlic, salt, pepper, sugar, and bay leaf. Pour tomatoes over this. Arrange thick slices of raw potatoes around skillet. Lay pork chops on top and cover with lid. Simmer for one hour.

Pork and Spaghetti Piccata

Joseph M. Amherd, Chef, Kansas City Union Station, Missouri

. . . .

1 lb. pork tenderloin,
sliced thin and flattened
1 teaspoon salt
1/8 teaspoon pepper
2 eggs, well beaten
1 1/4 cups butter
1 package (7 oz.) spaghetti
3/4 cup grated Swiss cheese
1/4 cup finely chopped chives

Season tenderloin slices with salt and pepper, dip in beaten egg, and sauté in 1/4 cup butter. Meanwhile cook spaghetti in boiling salted water and drain. Brown remaining cup of butter until dark and pour over spaghetti. Serve spaghetti on hot platter; arrange tenderloin slices over spaghetti; sprinkle with cheese and chives. Serves four.

Sweet-Sour Pork en Casserole

. . . .

1 1/2 lbs. pork cut in small cubes
1 1/2 cups pineapple juice
1/2 cup brown sugar
1 teaspoon soy sauce
1/2 cup flour
2 tablespoons shortening
Salt and pepper

Dredge pork in salt, pepper, and flour. Sauté in shortening until brown. Add remaining ingredients and simmer until well done. Serve in small casserole over steamed rice or chow mein noodles. Serves four.

Baked Ham with Kumquats and Yams

Nelle Smith, Test Kitchen Supervisor

· ·

4 ($^1/_4$" to $^1/_2$") slices
ready-to-eat ham
12 to 16 kumquats
2 large yams

Place ham slices in baking pan. Cut kumquats in half and place skin side up to form circle in center of ham. Place yams on top of kumquats. Place in 350-degree oven for 40-45 minutes.

Curry of Lamb

Hans Mayr, Chef, The Bowl and Bottle, Chicago, Illinois

2 lbs. leg of lamb
2 tablespoons fat
2 teaspoons salt
$1/4$ teaspoon pepper
$1/4$ cup chopped onion
3 tablespoons curry powder
About 2 cups water or stock
$1/4$ cup all-purpose flour
1 cup light cream
1 cup apple sauce

Ask meat dealer to slice lamb one inch thick; then chop into very thin pieces about an inch square, holding knife in a slanting position. Brown meat lightly in fat; season with salt and pepper. Remove meat from skillet, add onion and cook slowly until a light golden brown. Add curry powder and blend well. Return meat to skillet, add water or stock to barely cover meat, cover, and simmer until tender (1 $1/2$ to 2 hours). Blend flour with $1/4$ cup cold water; stir into hot mixture and cook until thickened, stirring constantly. Add cream and apple sauce and blend well. Serve immediately over fluffy rice. Serves five.

Ragout of Lamb Kidneys Piquante

Erich Walther, Santa Fe, New Mexico

12 lamb kidneys
$1/4$ cup butter
4 teaspoons finely chopped onion
2 cups beef bouillon
1 $1/2$ teaspoons dry mustard
Chopped parsley
2 tablespoons all-purpose flour
Dash pepper
3 tablespoons vinegar
(or 2 teaspoons concentrated meat
extract dissolved in 2 cups
boiling water)

Wash kidneys well and remove membranous covering. Split in half and remove white center. Slice thinly. Melt butter in frying pan. Add sliced kidneys and brown over high heat three or four minutes. Remove kidneys. Cook onions in butter until tender but not browned. Combine flour and mustard. Add to onions. Add bouillon and vinegar and cook until thickened. Remove from heat. Add kidneys and heat but do not boil. Add seasoning if needed. Sprinkle with chopped parsley just before serving. Serves four.

Rolled Rack of Lamb

Roland Mitlohner, Chef, Old Spinning Wheel, Hinsdale, Illinois

. . . .

1 4–lb. rack of lamb (with rib bones removed and fat trimmed away so that only the eye of the rib remains)
2 cloves garlic
$1/4$ lb. butter
1 tablespoon chopped parsley
5 slices of dried white bread
Salt and ground pepper to taste
Mustard paste (combine 2 teaspoons of Coleman's mustard with $1/4$ cup water)

Season rib eye with salt and freshly ground pepper. Bake in 400–degree oven until medium rare (30 to 45 minutes). Remove from oven. Baste lamb with mustard paste. Then take the pulp of the white bread and crush coarsely. Add to this freshly ground garlic, one teaspoon of salt and the chopped parsley. Mix thoroughly. Sprinkle the seasoned bread crumbs over lamb. Then glaze it with drawn butter and brown in hot oven (450 degrees). Serve with string beans and Lyonnaise potatoes. Serves six to eight people.

Lamb Chops à la Nelson

. . . .

Onions
Lambchop
Cheese
Tongue tips
Mushrooms

Make a dressing of boiled onions and grated cheese, passed through a sieve; broil chop on one side only, cover the unbroiled side with dressing and place in hot oven to brown; garnish with tongue tips and mushroom tops.

Chicken à la Marengo

George Burnickel, Chef, *California Limited*

Chicken
Salt and pepper
Mushrooms
Chicken stock
Garlic
Oil
Madeira wine
Herbs
Flour

Season washed, cut-up chicken pieces with salt and pepper, and fry in oil with herbs and garlic. When browned, place the chicken in another frying pan, then fry button mushrooms in the oil. Remove and place with the chicken. Pour surplus oil from pan, add flour, stir, and moisten with chicken stock and Madeira wine. Let it boil up, then skim and strain over the chicken. Simmer the chicken until tender. Serve garnished with mushrooms.

Breast of Chicken, Jeannette

Charles Zuellig, Chef, Alvarado Hotel, Albuquerque, New Mexico

Chicken breast
Pimentos
Foie-gras purée
Hard-boiled egg whites
Chaud-froid sauce
Olives
Lettuce

Remove the breast of a cooked fowl. Fill the breast with foie-gras purée (foie gras is a goose liver preparation) and trim to oval shape. Place on wire rack and coat with smooth, white chaud-froid sauce. Decorate as you desire with pimentos, whites of hard-boiled eggs, and olives cut in fancy shapes. Place in ice box until ready to use and serve on lettuce-lined plates.

Fried Chicken, Castañeda

Dan Tachet, Chef, Castañeda, Las Vegas, New Mexico

. . . .

1 3-lb. hen, sliced about
a third of an inch thick

Onion, chopped very fine

1 quart good chicken broth

Butter

Flour

$^1/_2$ pint cream

2 egg yolks

Parsley

Bread crumbs

Eggs

Fry the onion in butter, add flour, mix and pour in the broth and cream. Stir and let come to a boil. Let it cook about 10 minutes. Add egg yolks and parsley, and remove from the fire. This sauce must be quite thick. Dip the slices of chicken in the sauce so that it adheres to both sides. Lay them in a pan sprinkled with bread crumbs and also sprinkle the chicken with bread crumbs. When cold, dip them in beaten egg and crumbs and fry in deep hot grease. Serve with tomato sauce and French peas as garnish. (If handled properly, one three-pound hen will make 10 to 12 fair-sized orders.)

Chicken Maciel

Joseph Amherd, Chef, Kansas City Union Station, Missouri

. . . .

1 lb. cooked white meat of chicken

2 teaspoons curry powder

$^1/_4$ cup sherry

2 cups boiled rice

$^1/_4$ lb. butter

1 quart cream sauce, made with:

$^1/_2$ cup butter or chicken fat

$^1/_2$ cup flour

4 cups rich milk (part chicken broth)

Salt and pepper to taste

Grated Swiss cheese

Cut chicken into one-inch squares. Sauté five minutes in melted butter with curry powder and sherry. Fold chicken and rice into hot cream sauce and stir carefully until blended. Place in three individual casseroles (or one large casserole), sprinkle with grated Swiss cheese, and brown under broiler. Serves three.

Oven-Fried Chicken

Norton M. King, Chef, Kent County Airport, Michigan

· ·

3 Fryers, 2 1/2- to 3-lbs. each,
quartered
Salt and pepper to taste
1 cup flour
1/4 lb. butter, melted
Oil to cover bottom of roasting pan
Spiced peaches

Roll chicken in flour and brown in hot oil in roasting pan. When golden brown, brush with melted butter, sprinkle with salt and pepper, and bake in 350-degree oven until tender (45 minutes to one hour). Garnish with spiced peaches. Serves six.

Chicken Breast Tenerife
au Grand Marnier

Theodor Sonnenschein, Chef, Victor Hugo Inn, Laguna Beach, California

· ·

Boned chicken breast
Crushed whole almonds
Orange juice
Bread crumbs
Flour
Clarified butter
Eggs
Diced shrimp
Fresh papaya
Mushrooms
Grand Marnier
Perigueux Sauce

Marinate seasoned boneless chicken breast in orange juice overnight. Dry chicken breast; dip in flour, eggs, and a mixture of crushed white almonds and fresh white bread crumbs. Sauté very slowly in clarified butter. Serve on a bed of diced shrimp, fresh papaya, and mushrooms, sautéed in butter and flamed with Grand Marnier. Serve Perigueux Sauce with a taste of Grand Marnier on the side.

Jellied Chicken

Fred Wendell, Inspector

. . . .

Chicken (with feet)
Salt and pepper

Cook a young fowl slowly until tender. Take the meat from the bones and continue to cook the bones until they fall apart. Let the liquid stand until it is cold. Remove all fat, reheat it, and season with salt and pepper. Put into it the meat, turn into a mold and set away to get cold. The meat should be in small pieces. To insure a stiff jelly, boil the chicken feet with the bones. First scald them and draw off the outside skin like a stocking, then cut off the ends of the toes and the tops of the legs just below the joints. There is a cupful of stiff jelly in a pair of chicken feet. Season the jelly to suit taste.

Chicken Cacciatore

Louis Sogno, Chef, Los Angeles Union Station, California

. . . .

2 broiling chickens (1 $^1/_2$ lbs. each,
ready-to-eat weight)
1 can tomato purée (or 1 cup
canned tomatoes)
$^1/_2$ cup flour
1 teaspoon salt
$^1/_8$ teaspoon pepper
$^1/_4$ cup butter or olive oil
1 medium onion, sliced
$^1/_2$ lb. fresh mushrooms, sliced
1 clove garlic, minced
12 ripe olives, whole
$^1/_2$ cup claret or sherry

Cut chicken in quarters, and dust with flour which has been well mixed with salt and pepper. Sauté in butter or olive oil until golden brown. Add remaining ingredients, cover, and simmer over low heat 20 to 30 minutes. Serves four.

Chicken Vesuvio

John Garozzo, Chef, Chicago Union Station, Illinois

Half of 2 ¹/₂ lb. chicken
cut into four pieces
Salt to taste
Garlic powder to taste
¹/₄ cup olive oil
3 oz. dry white wine
1 Idaho potato cut into 6 pieces
lengthwise
MSG to taste
1 teaspoon oregano
Flour

Sprinkle salt and garlic powder over the chicken. Flour the chicken. Heat olive oil in pan (no wood or plastic handles on pan). Add floured chicken; brown on both sides. Remove chicken from pan and add potatoes. When potatoes are browned, add chicken again to pan with potatoes. Now, add oregano, a little more garlic powder, and salt. Stir and put into preheated 425-degree oven for about 30 minutes (until potatoes and chicken are done.) When done, remove pan from oven. Add about three ounces white wine (have cover ready). Let simmer a few minutes on the stove. Arrange chicken on plate with potatoes on top. Season to taste (more garlic, oregano, etc.) Pour sauce over chicken and potatoes.

Breast of Chicken El Tovar

James Marques, Chef

6 whole breasts of chicken, cooked
6 large mushrooms
1 ounce Sherry wine
1 pint half-and-half
Wild rice, cooked
Hollandaise Sauce

Cook mushrooms lightly in sherry. Add half-and-half. Cook down to a thick sauce. Arrange cooked chicken breasts on wild rice in baking dish. Pour over sherry and mushrooms. Glaze with Hollandaise Sauce. Place in hot oven until chicken is golden brown. Serves six.

Chicken Sauté Robert with Goufrette Potatoes

Robert Shinn, Chef, Old Spinning Wheel Restaurant, Hinsdale, Illinois

. . . .

1 small frying chicken (2 to 2 ^{1}/$_2$ lbs.)

Egg

^{1}/$_2$ cup sherry

4 large peeled raw potatoes

2 tablespoons butter

8 large fresh mushroom caps

Seasoned flour

Milk

Shortening

Disjoint chicken and roll in seasoned flour. Dip in egg-milk mixture; roll again in flour. Melt butter in a heavy skillet, but do not brown. Drop in chicken; cook until golden brown. Remove chicken to a covered pan and place in moderate oven until done (about 30 minutes). Small amount of water may be added for steaming. With waffle-edge knife, slice potatoes very thin turning them a one-quarter turn at each slice. Wash slices, then drain and cook in shortening ^{1}/$_2$ inch deep. In the pan used to brown chicken, add mushroom caps sliced very thin. Cook until tender, add wine and cook until volume is reduced by half. Remove chicken from oven and place in casserole dish. Arrange potatoes around the edge and pour in wine and mushroom liquid. Return to oven and heat until bubbling hot. Serves two to four.

Fried Chicken

Nelle Smith, Test Kitchen Supervisor

. . . .

1 chicken, disjointed

Prepare and fry your chicken as usual. The chicken may be fried ahead of time and refrigerated. Wrap fried chicken loosely in foil paper; overlap edges and lock ends. Place package on grill over coals; turn often. Allow 30 to 35 minutes to heat.

Wild Canadian Goose

Heinz Rauschenbach, Chef, Chicago Union Station, Illinois

1 goose (7 to 10 lbs.)

4 to 5 slices bacon

2 medium-sized apples

2 bay leaves

2 cloves

Dash thyme

1 onion

2 cups beef stock

Juniper berries

2 cups chicken stock

3 stalks celery, diced

3 tablespoons flour

2 sprigs parsley

3 tablespoons butter, softened

2 onions, diced

2 tablespoons cognac

3 carrots, diced

Quarter apples and insert cloves into onion. Stuff goose with apples, onion, one stalk of diced celery, juniper berries, and parsley. Tie legs together and salt. Place goose in roasting pan and cover with bacon. Roast in a 400-degree oven for about 25 to 30 minutes or until lightly browned. Then reduce heat to 350 degrees and remove bacon slices. Add bay leaves, thyme, remaining celery, carrots, and onions to roasting pan. When the vegetables are browned, add beef and chicken stock. Continue roasting (20 minutes to the pound) until tender. Remove goose from roasting pan and sauté remaining vegetables for five minutes more. Add cognac and simmer until liquid is reduced to half. Season with salt and pepper. Blend together three tablespoons flour and butter (beurre manié); bring sauce to a boil and thicken. Boil a few minutes more and put sauce through sieve. Serve hot with goose. Serves eight.

Barbecued Chicken

. . . .

2 chickens, 2 ¹/₂ to 3 ¹/₂ lb.each,
including neck, gizzard, heart
1 sliced onion
2 cloves garlic, sliced

Sauce

1 large sliced onion
2 teaspoons bacon drippings
1 cup cold water
1 teaspoon salt
¹/₄ teaspoon black pepper
2 bouillon cubes
1 small can tomato paste
Worcestershire sauce
¹/₄ teaspoon black thyme

Have the butcher quarter the chickens; that's easier than wrassling with them yourself. Clean, salt, and store in the refrigerator for several hours before cooking. Then lay pieces, skin side down, in a shallow open pan. Add sliced onion, gizzards, hearts and garlic. Pour in water to fill pan ³/₄ inch. Cook in moderately hot oven (325 degrees) for one hour, turning occasionally; water should be reduced by about half. As soon as chicken is in the oven, prepare barbecue sauce. Brown the diced onion in bacon drippings. Add cold water gradually so fat doesn't sputter. When thoroughly heated, add salt and pepper, then the bouillon cubes; stir until they are dissolved. Add tomato paste, a dash of Worcestershire to taste, and black thyme (you can get this from the drugstore if your grocer doesn't carry it). The sauce may be prepared in advance (be smart and double the proportions for two occasions); if you do prepare it early, reheat it to boiling, and when the chicken has cooked for half an hour pour all the sauce over it. Baste with the hot sauce every ten minutes, leaving a pool of sauce in the rib cage when halves are turned up. Cook until chicken is tender and sauce reduced to a rich gravy. Should the sauce thicken before chicken is done, add ¹/₂ cup to one cup boiling water at a time. Lift chicken to hot platter and serve the sauce separately. Eight quarters.

Breast of Chicken Lucrecio

. . . .

5-lb. hen
Fat for frying
1 tablespoon pickling spice
Flour
¹/3 cup chili powder
Chicken stock
²/3 cup flour
¹/4 lb. almonds
Butter

Cut a five-pound hen in serving pieces. Place in deep kettle, entirely cover with hot water, and season with one tablespoon mixed pickling spices. Bring water slowly to boiling then reduce heat and simmer until tender, about 2 ¹/2 hours. Remove breast and roll it in mixture of ¹/3 cup chili powder and ²/3 cup flour. Fry in shallow fat until golden brown, then remove. Make a gravy by adding flour to the fat and gradually adding chicken stock. Return chicken breast to pan and let simmer about 20 minutes, stirring gravy frequently. Pour gravy over the hot chicken breast on platter. The legs may also be used the same way. While chicken is simmering, blanch ¹/4 pound almonds, shred or chop coarsely; brown in butter and sprinkle over the chicken just before serving. Serve Posole with the chicken. Serves four.

Chicken Poulette

Chester Gerlich, Chef, Harvey House, Riverside Plaza, Chicago, Illinois

. . . .

2 cups white meat chicken, diced
¹/4 lb. butter
2 tablespoons shallots
¹/2 cup diced mushrooms
¹/4 cup white wine
2 cups cream
1 tablespoon chives, chopped
1 cup Sauce Supreme

Melt butter in skillet and sauté shallots on low fire till clear. Add mushrooms and again sauté till clear; do not brown. Add chicken and wine and heat thoroughly. Add cream, Sauce Supreme, and chives and simmer for about five minutes. Serve in chafing dish or patty shell.

Braised Duck Cumberland

Joseph Stoesser, Chef, *Super Chief*

· ·

1 duck, 5 to 6 lbs.

Salt and pepper

1/4 cup chopped onion

3 tablespoons butter

2 1/2 cups boiling chicken broth

1 cup rice

1/4 cup butter

1/2 teaspoon salt

1 large stalk celery

1 large carrot

1 small onion

1 cup water

Sauce

1 teaspoon all-purpose flour

1 cup bouillon

1 large orange

1/3 cup Burgundy wine

1/4 teaspoon English mustard

Dash cayenne

1 teaspoon Worcestershire sauce

1 tablespoon currant jelly

Season cavity of duck with salt and pepper. To make stuffing: cook chopped onion in butter until tender; add rice and cook until rice turns yellow. Add chicken broth, butter, and salt, cover, and simmer 20 minutes. Stuff duck with mixture and truss. Place duck on trivet in roasting pan, breast up. Add celery stalk, whole carrot, onion and water. Cook in slow oven (325 degrees) 25 minutes per pound (about 2 1/2 hours) basting duck occasionally. Remove duck from pan; drain off excess fat. Sprinkle flour in pan, add bouillon, and simmer about 20 minutes, stirring occasionally; strain. Peel orange, remove zest, and cut or peel into thin strips. Boil five minutes, drain, and add to hot mixture with wine, mustard, Worcestershire sauce, jelly, and cayenne. Separate orange into sections removing white membrane. Place duck on serving platter; arrange orange sections in two rows over duck. Pour a few spoonsful of sauce over all. Serve remaining sauce with duck.

Chicken Enchiladas

Dan Tachet, Chef, Castañeda, Las Vegas, New Mexico

. . . .

1 quart sauce, ¹/₂ chile and
¹/₂ tomatoes, lightly sweetened
1 hen, diced
3 to 4 chopped onions
10 olives cut in half
3 oz. cheese, grated
1 teaspoon marjoram

Mix the diced chicken with a little of the chili sauce, onion, and cheese. Add a teaspoonful of marjoram and a little salt. Put the tortillas on a table, covering each one with a spoonful of the mixture. Roll them like a pancake, trim the edges, put them in a greased pan and sprinkle some grated cheese upon them. Leave them in the oven long enough to be hot but not crisp. Serve with chili sauce and decorate with olives.

2 cups flour
1 cup Cream of Wheat
Water
1 spoonful lard
Salt
Egg

Tortillas

Mix well into a thin pouring batter and fry the same as French pancakes. Makes 10.

SEAFOOD

Finnan Haddie, Dearborn

Chicago Union Station, Illinois

1 lb. finnan haddie
1 ¹/₂ cups milk
2 medium potatoes,
cooked and cut in thick slices
Melted butter
1 cup cream
Paprika
Parsley

Simmer fish in milk for 10 minutes. Place in two individual shallow casseroles or shirred egg dishes. Arrange potato slices at one end of casserole. Brush potatoes with butter, sprinkle with salt. Pour cream over fish and potatoes, sprinkle with paprika. Bake in moderate oven (350 degrees) for 15 minutes. Sprinkle with parsley if desired. Cover casserole to retain the wonderful aroma, and serve immediately, hot and bubbly. Serves two.

Shrimp à la Marquez

Furnace Creek Inn and Ranch, Death Valley, California

¹/₂ bell pepper
¹/₂ onion
1 shallot
3 stalks celery
1 peeled tomato
1 clove garlic
3 oz. sherry
1 lb. shrimp
1 ¹/₂ pints 20 percent cream
1 tablespoon raw spinach
Wild rice, cooked

Chop the pepper, onion, spinach, shallot, celery, tomato, and garlic fine and sauté them in butter. Then add the sherry, shrimp, and cream. Cook until the cream is reduced and thick. Serve en casserole with wild rice. Serves six.

Salmon Steaks with Mustard Sauce

Manfred Gunter Westerwelle, Chef, Victor Hugo Inn, Laguna Beach, California

. . . .

2 egg yolks
^{1}/2 teaspoon salt
1 teaspoon dry mustard
1 cup olive oil
2 tablespoons tarragon white vinegar
1 teaspoon Dijon mustard
^{1}/2 teaspoon sugar
2 tablespoons chopped dill
Salmon steaks
Butter
Parsley

Beat two egg yolks, and add one teaspoon dry mustard, one teaspoon Dijon mustard, ^{1}/2 teaspoon sugar, and ^{1}/2 teaspoon salt. Mix ingredients well. Beat in slowly one cup of olive oil as you would do for mayonnaise; add two tablespoons of tarragon wine vinegar and two tablespoons chopped dill. Serve salmon steaks right from the broiler. Put a pat of cold butter mixed with chopped dill and parsley on top of each steak and serve mustard sauce on the side.

Grilled Marinated Salmon

Manfred Gunter Westerwelle

. . . .

3 lbs. salmon steaks, 1" thick
12 stalks fresh dill, chopped
^{1}/4 cup salt
1 teaspoon ground pepper
3 tablespoons sugar

Put three pounds of raw salmon steak in a shallow bowl. Cover with ^{1}/4 cup salt, three full tablespoons sugar, about 12 fresh stalks chopped dill, and one teaspoon freshly ground pepper. Rub mixture into salmon and be sure it is thoroughly coated, then let it stand in refrigerator for 36 hours. Place salmon under very hot broiler, close to the flame, and grill three minutes on each side.

Lobster Americaine

Carlos Gardini, Chef, *Super Chief*

. . . .

1 2-lb. lobster, boiled

3 tablespoons butter

1 tablespoon minced celery

1 teaspoon minced carrots

1 teaspoon minced leeks

1 teaspoon minced shallots

$^1/_2$ garlic clove, minced

2 tablespoons cognac

2 tablespoons flour

$^1/_4$ cup broth

2 tablespoons white wine

2 tomatoes, peeled and chopped

Dash salt

Dash pepper

Dash cayenne pepper

1 tablespoon butter

Remove meat from shell (saving the brain) and cut in pieces an inch thick. Melt butter, add minced vegetables, and sauté several minutes without browning. Add lobster meat and garlic and continue sautéing for five minutes. Add cognac and set aflame. Blend in the flour, add broth, and stir until smooth and slightly thickened. Add wine and chopped tomatoes, season to taste, and cook slowly for 20 minutes. Mix brain with softened butter, add to lobster mixture and serve at once. Serves one.

Shrimp Maciel

Joe Maciel

. . . .

10 deveined cooked shrimp

1 oz. sherry

1 level teaspoon curry powder

1 cup boiled rice, colored yellow

1 pint medium-thick cream sauce

3 oz. butter

1 $^1/_2$ oz. grated Swiss cheese

Melt butter and sauté shrimp with sherry and curry for five minutes. Add cream sauce and bring to a boil. Line casserole or chafing dish with rice; pour shrimp mixture over rice; top with grated Swiss cheese; and place under broiler until lightly browned. Serves one.

Pompano en Papillote

Paul Martin, Chef, Sunport, Albuquerque, New Mexico

. . . .

4 filets of pompano
Dash of Maggi
2 cups dry sherry
¹/4 cup cooked mushrooms
¹/4 cup Bechamel sauce
Melted butter
¹/4 cup Hollandaise Sauce
¹/4 cup whipped cream

Poach four filets of pompano in two cups dry sherry for five to seven minutes, or until tender to touch of a fork. Remove from the liquid, set aside, and keep warm. Mix ¹/4 cup hot Bechamel sauce with ¹/4 cup Hollandaise Sauce and ¹/4 cup whipped cream, dash of Maggi; add ¹/4 cup drained cooked mushrooms and blend. Cut heart shape from parchment or silicone paper. Lay flat and brush with melted butter, put half the sauce on the right center of the paper, the poached filets on the sauce, the remainder of the sauce over the filets. Fold left side over to meet the right and from the top of the heart make a series of folds until you reach the point; then twist the point and press down. Put folded side down on greased baking dish, brush top of package with butter and bake in 375 degree oven until package puffs and is golden brown. Serve at once in the paper with parsley potatoes. Serves four.

Fruit de Mer, Madame Pompadour

Carl Burger, Chef, Palmolive Building Restaurants, Chicago, Illinois

. . . .

6 filets of sole, 6 oz. each

18 cooked shrimp

2 cooked lobster tails,
each cut in 6 slices

12 mushroom caps, cooked slowly
in a little butter

1 shallot

Parsley

White wine

Salt and pepper

Grated Parmesan cheese

Season filets with salt and pepper. Cut them into two-inch strips. Fold over to make into a roll and lay filets in the bottom of a generously buttered earthenware or baking dish. Sprinkle with 1 1/2 tablespoons finely chopped shallots and cover with white wine. Add a few sprigs of parsley. Bring to a boil over medium flame; cover the dish with buttered paper and bake in moderate oven for ten minutes. Drain the liquid from the baking dish into a saucepan to make Sauce Chantilly. Arrange filets in the casserole and place between them the shrimp and slices of lobster tail. Place mushroom caps on top. Cover with Sauce Chantilly. Sprinkle very lightly with grated Parmesan cheese; brown under the broiler and serve. Serves six.

Coconut Mahi-mahi "Aloha"

Fred Adler, Chef, Music Center Restaurants, Los Angeles, California

. . . .

3 lbs. fresh or frozen mahi-mahi filet

Meat of 1 fresh young coconut
(whites only), ground

1 glass (6 oz.) dry Sauterne wine

Juice of 1 coconut

Juice of 2 limes

2 oz. chopped shallots

2 cups fish stock or clam juice

2 oz. butter

2 lbs. cooked leaf spinach

Salt and pepper

5 oz. cream

Duchesse potatoes

Hollandaise Sauce

Whipping cream

Cut mahi-mahi in six- or seven-ounce portions. Sprinkle shallots in well-buttered stainless steel pan or sautoire. Arrange fish side by side. Pour wine, lime juice, ground coconut, and fish stock over fish, then season with salt and pepper. Cover fish with buttered wax paper and poach in the oven for about 10 minutes. Drain off liquid and use it to make a fish sauce (Veloute), adding five ounces table cream to sauce. Cook for 20 minutes and then strain. Take eight large, cleaned coconut shells (halves cut lengthwise), and put one serving portion of sautéed leaf spinach in each shell. Put fish on top, then cover with the prepared sauce. Make a border with duchesse potatoes around inner shell top. Finally top with "Royal" ($2/3$ Hollandaise Sauce and $1/3$ unsweetened whipped cream, both blended together). Bake under broiler until golden brown.

Ragout of Rabbit

Johann Mayr, Chef, Palmolive Building, Chicago, Illinois

1 rabbit, skinned
1 pint stock
Salt and pepper
$1/2$ lb. pearl onions
Flour
$1/2$ lb. spiced mushrooms
Paprika
$1/2$ pint sour cream
Shortening
Cornstarch (optional)

Once the rabbit is skinned, cleaned, and cut in pieces, add salt and pepper. Then roll in a mixture of flour with a little paprika. Fry to a golden brown in bacon drippings or any shortening. Add stock, pearl onions, and spiced mushrooms. Boil, and then simmer slowly in a covered casserole. When the rabbit is done, add sour cream; let this stew come to a good boil. Season to taste. You may wish to thicken this gravy with cornstarch. Don't strain the gravy. Serve with wild or domestic rice or spaghetti.

CHAPTER FIVE

The Harvey Girls

. . . .

It was in 1883 that Fred Harvey implemented the staff-development policy that would be his greatest impact on the American West. In later years a manager named Tom Gable alleged that *he* had made the suggestion to recruit women servers from the East. Gable had suddenly been installed as the manager of the Raton, New Mexico, Harvey House, when the previous staff was fired en masse the morning after a fight had rendered some of the waiters unable to work due to their "carved up" condition. As fate would have it, the morning after the fight Harvey made an inspection stop and cleaned house.

Advertisements appeared shortly thereafter in a number of eastern and midwestern newspapers:

> **WANTED:** Young women, 18 to 30 years of age, of good character, attractive and intelligent.

And a number of attractive, intelligent young women of good character responded. Those who survived an initial screening became the first "Harvey Girls"—a title Harvey insisted must replace "waitress." Not surprisingly, the overall level of service went up, as did the general level and tone of behavior in the Harvey Houses.

The Harvey Girls were, indeed, required to be of good character. Their past private lives were probed to an extent that would bring on an avalanche of civil rights lawsuits against personnel departments today. The screening process removed most of the doubtful cases at the beginning, with only the attractive, intelligent, and chaste allowed to proceed westward for training. Starting out, they were paid $17.50 a

Perhaps the most unusual "Harvey House" was the one that floated on San Francisco Bay. The passenger ferry Ocean Wave connected San Francisco with Santa Fe trains at the railroad's Richmond terminal, across the Bay. While there is no record that Fred Harvey ever operated anything larger than a newsstand in the San Francisco Ferry Building, the dining facilities on the ferry itself featured Fred Harvey service which, in the opinion of many travelers, put the food service of the rival Southern Pacific to shame on a daily basis. (Colorado Historical Society)

month, plus room, board, and tips, a package comparable to prevailing wage rates. Their meals, of course, were unsurpassed, and living quarters were in a dormitory adjacent to or above the restaurant. Curfew was 10:00 P.M., overseen by a more senior Harvey Girl who had worked her way up to become a housemother and supervisor.

Their dress was designed to diminish, rather than accentuate, feminine physical characteristics. Black and white uniforms, skirts eight inches from the floor (no more, no less), with "Elsie" collars. Black stockings (opaque), black shoes (comfortable). Hair in a net, tied with a regulation white ribbon. No makeup. Faces were periodically checked by the housemother with a damp towel.

In spite of these cosmetic restrictions, the impact of a few "good, attractive, and intelligent" women on a small western town is difficult to understate. The number of local customers rose gratifyingly, and the old problem of male waiters fighting or in other ways rendering themselves unfit for duty disappeared. The women, too, found that though "waitresses" were looked down upon, Harvey Girls were not! It

A typical scene between trains in a Harvey House lunchroom. Harvey Girls clean up, prepare for the next group of passengers, and prepare another urn of famous Fred Harvey coffee. (Santa Fe Collections, Kansas State Historical Society)

took an acknowledged skill to serve sixteen people (the per-station average) in twenty-five minutes.

Although most men proved themselves to be substandard in this line of work, one exception allowed some to keep their jobs. Black male waiters remained in place in Harvey Houses on the California desert because of a popular belief that Negroes were better suited to the heat. The group at Needles distinguished itself as a gospel chorus, meeting every train with a hymn.

One liability to hiring attractive women lured in from the East was the good chance that they would soon marry and quit their jobs. Thus the Harvey Girls were required to sign contracts for a year's service, and to forfeit half their base pay if they married before one year had elapsed. Marriage was always on the horizon, or closer; there simply weren't many unmarried females in the West "of good character, attractive and intelligent" besides the Harvey Girls. They were greatly outnumbered by men, upon whom they had a remarkable impact.

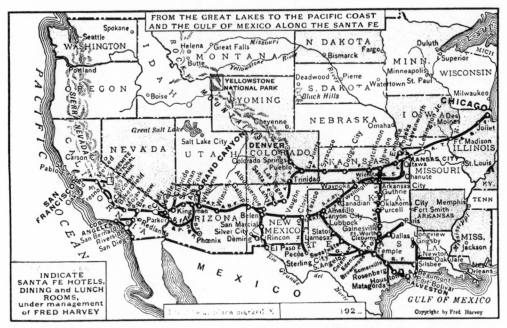

The Fred Harvey–Santa Fe empire covered eleven states and became the best-known western railroad route in America. This timetable map shows the major Fred Harvey installations at the height of operations in the 1920s, but it is slightly misleading, in that it identifies several California communities in which there were only newsstands, not lunch rooms or dining rooms.

In fact, it was commonly stated around the turn of the century that Fred Harvey's best "dish" was the Harvey Girl. Behold a poem written by a Californian named J. C. Davis in 1895:

> *Harvey Houses, don't you savvy;*
> *clean across the ole Mojave,*
> *On the Santa Fe they've strung 'em*
> *like a string of Indian beads.*
> *We all couldn't eat without 'em,*
> *but the slickest thing about 'em*
> *Is the Harvey skirts that hustle up the feeds.*

Literally thousands of Harvey Girls ended their restaurant careers by marrying men in western towns. They then turned their attentions to improving those communities. As they married and matured, the eastern cultural instincts of these fomer Harvey Girls led them to organize civic activity for improved safety and quality of life. Theirs were the voices in the forefront of "Law and Order" movements designed to reduce gun-fighting incidents. Their voices were also the ones most likely to be heard lifted in song in the choir lofts of newly built churches, or on

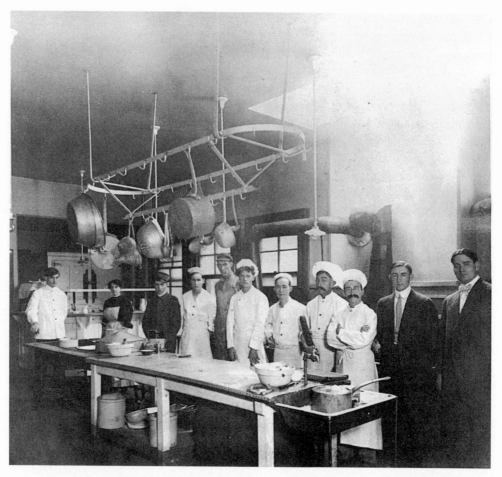

The Harvey Girl service was supported by a rarely photographed but vital kitchen staff and restaurant management, assembled here between trains. These chefs took inordinate pride in their work, even in the remotest part of the desert. (Santa Fe Collections, Kansas State Historical Society)

makeshift stages from which recitals were presented to the community. The retired Harvey Girls were at the forefront of civic improvement activities of all kinds, and the communities flourished in ways that they never would have had the job been left to men alone.

The Harvey influence revealed itself in another way too. Elbert Hubbard once whimsically claimed that more than four thousand boys born to these couples were named Fred, or Harvey, or both. The reality was that the Harvey Girls who married and settled in the West tended to marry men of high standing and to be the most capable women in the community. They did, indeed, become the West's "aristocracy."

Besides the fine food and charming women, another ingredient of the Harvey influence was reading matter. Since the first trains ran, "news butchers" had prowled the aisles of cars with an assortment of merchandise: newspapers, books, candy, cigars, and other assorted items for the traveler. As with the trackside restaurants, the quality of these items usually was inferior, and they were grossly overpriced. "Dirty boys selling dirty books, dirty candy and cheap cigars" was one description.

In 1897, a Santa Fe Railroad vice president decided to upgrade the newsstand and news-butcher operation. The Fred Harvey organization was called upon to operate the station newsstands and on-train concessions for the Santa Fe, and the standards improved immediately. Candy and tobacco were fresh, and the train vendors were trained not to be. The Harvey concessions division grew to encompass on-train sales and more than a hundred station newsstands, as well as an array of specialty shops in the larger railroad stations. While it provided immediate consumable items, the concession also had a long-lasting effect by improving the quality and assortment of available books and magazines, including classic and popular literature and magazines for all tastes.

Perhaps more than any other individual, Fred Harvey helped civilize the American West. His impact was manifold, broader even than his vast contribution to the rail dining experience. Upgrading the railway newsstands, he introduced better reading material into the culture. He established a standard of service that, though demanding of the staff, was respectful to customers and kept luring them back. Not least, he wooed westward more than five thousand "good" women who not only helped keep his restaurants afloat but shaped the region's culture and attitudes. The taste of a fine steak might last a day, but the enchantment of the Harvey Girls lingered on and on.

Rice & Pasta

Risotto, Piedmontaise

Louis Sogno, Chef, Union Station, Los Angeles, California

. . . .

1 small onion, chopped fine
4 tablespoons butter
1 cup rice
1/2 teaspoon salt
2 1/2 cups chicken broth, heated to boiling
Grated Parmesan cheese

Sauté minced onion in butter to a golden brown. Add uncooked rice and continue heating until rice is browned slightly, about 10 minutes, stirring constantly. Add salt and boiling chicken broth; cover, reduce heat to low, and cook slowly for 18 to 20 minutes or until rice is tender and excess liquid has evaporated. Serve hot, topped or mixed with grated Parmesan cheese. Serves four.

Spaghetti with Chestnuts
(Lenten Dish)

. . . .

Chestnuts
Cooked spaghetti
Butter
Milk
Chopped onions
Grated Cheddar cheese

Roast the chestnuts, peel, and pass them through a sieve. Mix with the spaghetti; add some chopped onions. Pour over melted butter and milk to smother, sprinkle with grated Cheddar cheese, and bake au gratin.

Spaghetti Incasciati
(Hidden Spaghetti)

(A typical Italian dish, of which Brillat-Savarin in his
"Physiologie du gout" wrote with enthusiasm.)

. . . .

Strong beef tea

Sliced, sautéed eggplant

Tomato purée

Mushrooms, thinly sliced

Cooked spaghetti

Cooked cockscomb

Parmesan cheese

Prepare a strong beef tea with tomato purée. Pour some spaghetti in a deep dish; add some Parmesan cheese and beef tea. Then place a layer of the eggplant, fresh mushrooms, cooked cockscomb, and Parmesan cheese. Pour beef tea over this again and so on until the dish is filled. Bake about 10 minutes in oven, and serve immediately.

Spaghetti à la Vittorio

. . . .

Cooked chicken and sweetbreads

Grated Swiss cheese

Cooked, buttered spaghetti

Prepare chicken and sweetbreads in the manner of tetrazzini, pour in chafing dish (about one-third full), and place a high heap of buttered spaghetti in the center; sprinkle with grated, green Swiss cheese and bake to a nice brown.

Spaghetti à la Aida

. . . .

Diced ham

Chopped, fresh tomatoes

Chopped onions

Tomato sauce

Garlic

New peas

Spaghetti

Sauté some diced ham, chopped onions, and a little garlic. Add chopped, fresh tomatoes; fill up with tomato sauce and let reduce. Then add new peas and pour this entire mixture over the spaghetti.

Spaghetti à la Bolognaise

Beef tenderloin, minced
Tomato purée
Onions
Cooked, buttered spaghetti
Garlic
Grated Swiss cheese
Bordelaise Sauce
Tomato Sauce

Sauté minced beef tenderloin with onions and garlic, and fill up with Bordelaise Sauce (red wine). Thicken this with purée of tomatoes and season well. Place the buttered spaghetti in the center of a large, oblong-shaped au gratin bowl, place the prepared meat on each side of the spaghetti, and make a ring of grated green Swiss cheese around the meat. Bake lightly for a few minutes and serve at once with Tomato Sauce on the side.

Spaghetti à la Nicotera

Veal kidney
Tomatoes concassée
Beef tenderloin
Sherry
Mushrooms
Spaghetti
Parmesan cheese

Prepare well-seasoned ragout of veal kidneys, beef tenderloin, fresh mushrooms, and tomatoes concassée; deglaze with sherry wine. Serve it in a deep dish in layers with spaghetti and Parmesan cheese.

Spaghetti à la Dominicaine

Cooked spaghetti
Anchovy paste
Mushrooms

Serve the spaghetti, adding a thin purée of mushrooms and anchovy paste to chafing dish.

Stuffed Macaroni

Cooked macaroni
Madeira sauce
Goose liver
Truffles

Cut the macaroni in pieces of about four inches in length and open them, then prepare a farce (stuffing) of goose liver and truffles, fill by means of a tube, close them up, arrange the pieces nicely on a deep platter, pour some Madeira sauce over them, and let the whole heat well in an oven.

Macaroni à la Sicilienne

Cooked macaroni
Sautéed eggplant en Julienne
Grated cheese
Julienned mushrooms
Tomato purée
Cooked cockscomb
Grated cheese
Tomato sauce

Place a layer of cooked macaroni on a deep platter, add grated cheese, then purée of tomatoes, sautéed eggplant en Julienne, one layer of julienned mushrooms, cooked cockscomb, grated cheese, tomato sauce, and another layer of macaroni. Heat in oven.

Timbale of Macaroni Neapolitaine

Cooked macaroni
Quartered tomatoes
Bechamel sauce
Grated cheese

Butter the timbale and fill with the following preparation: mix macaroni with Bechamel and cheese, place a few quartered tomatoes in the middle of timbale, fill up with macaroni, and bake in oven.

Macaroni with Flaked Ham Au Gratin

. . . .

Cooked macaroni
Salt and pepper
Nutmeg
Bechamel Sauce
Grated Parmesan cheese
Ham flakes
Melted butter

Mix the macaroni proportionately with Bechamel (cream sauce), then add the thinly flaked and previously heated ham flakes; season with salt, pepper, and nutmeg; serve individually in casseroles au gratin. Sprinkle with grated Parmesan cheese and add a few drops of melted butter.

Macaroni Pudding à la Parisienne

. . . .

Cooked macaroni
Fricassee Sauce
Chicken
Eggs, separated
Ham

Cut the macaroni in small pieces, then add some white meat of chicken and ham chopped fine and mixed with Fricassee Sauce. To insure solidity, add the yolks and beaten whites of a few eggs, put the mixture in a pudding form, and bake in boiling water (bain marie).

Macaroni à la Milanaise

Ham
Tongue
Mushrooms en julienne
Purée of tomatoes
Butter
Chopped onions
Garlic
Macaroni, cooked
Chicken broth
Grated Parmesan cheese

Sauté the ham, tongue and mushrooms, in butter, with some finely chopped onions and a little garlic. Add the tomato purée and reduce. Work in the macaroni, which has been cut into two-inch pieces. Moisten, to taste, with chicken broth. Just before serving, sprinkle grated Parmesan cheese over the top.

Macaroni à la Montgelas

Cooked macaroni
Mushrooms
Butter
Chicken
Truffles
Tongue en julienne
Salt and pepper
Nutmeg

The macaroni is to be lightly sautéed in butter, then mixed with truffles, mushrooms, white meat of chicken, and tongue en julienne. Season with salt, pepper, and a little nutmeg.

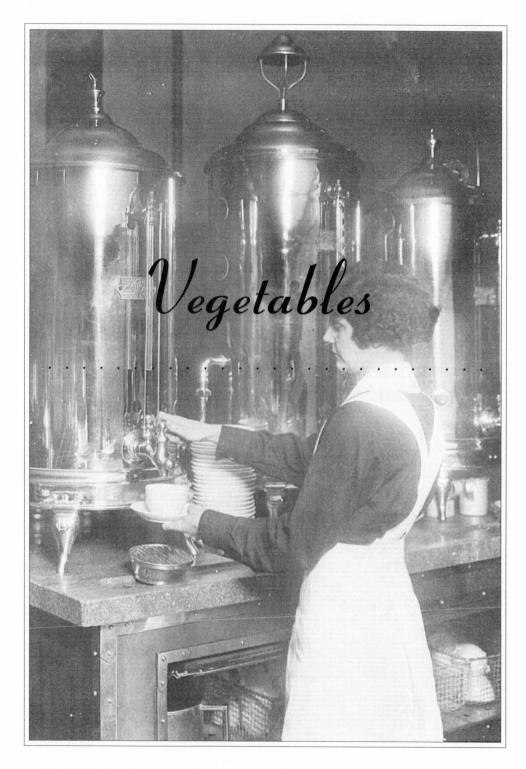

Vegetables

Stuffed Zucchini Andalouse

Carlos Gardini, Chef, *Super Chief*

. . . .

6 small zucchini

2 tablespoons chopped onion

$1/3$ cup chopped tomato

$1/4$ cup chopped cooked ham

$1/2$ clove garlic, minced

$1/2$ cup chopped cooked beef

3 tablespoons chopped mushrooms

3 tablespoons chopped green pepper

1 $1/3$ cup soft bread crumbs,
piled lightly

2 tablespoons broth, if needed

Dash of salt

Dash of pepper

Cook zucchini in unsalted water for five minutes; cut in half lengthwise; remove pulp. Combine pulp with remaining ingredients; pile this into zucchini and bake in moderate oven (350 degrees) for 30 minutes. Serves six.

Baked Tomatoes, Plain

Dan Tachet, Chef, Castañeda, Las Vegas, New Mexico

. . . .

Tomatoes

Butter

Bread crumbs

Use very firm tomatoes and peel them by dipping them into boiling water. Season and put them in a pan with plenty of bread crumbs sprinkled over them. Have a small lump of butter on top of each one and put them in a very hot oven. Brown, but do not have them mushy.

Cauliflower Greens, Restelli

Victor Restelli, Sous Chef, St. Louis Union Station, Missouri

. . . .

2 tablespoons chopped onion
3 strips bacon, diced
2 teaspoons olive oil
$^1/_2$ cup chopped tomatoes
$^1/_2$ cup tomato purée
$^1/_2$ clove garlic, minced
1 (1 $^1/_4$ lb.) head cauliflower
Grated Parmesan cheese (optional)

Sauté onion and bacon in olive oil until tender but not brown. Add chopped tomatoes, tomato purée, and garlic. Simmer until amount is reduced to half, about 20 minutes. Wash cauliflower, including the good leaves and stems, and chop fine. Cook five minutes in boiling salted water and drain. Add tomato sauce and serve. Sprinkle grated Parmesan cheese over each serving if desired. Serves four to six.

Roasting Ears

Nelle Smith, Test Kitchen Supervisor

. . . .

Corn
Salt and pepper
Butter

Turn back husks; remove silk. Pull husks back in place. Lay on grill over hot coals; turn ears of corn often. Allow 25 to 30 minutes to cook. For those who like a real sweet corn, let corn cook a little longer—kernels turn a taffy color. To serve: Pull husks back (hold ear with towel or wear gloves). Have loads of fresh butter and salt and pepper handy.

Chiles Rellenos à la Konrad

Konrad Allgaier, Chef, La Fonda Hotel, Santa Fe, New Mexico

. . . .

8 canned Ortega chili peppers
$^1/_2$ cup flour
1 egg beaten
Butter
$^1/_2$ cup grated aged American cheese

Fill each chili pepper with one tablespoon cheese. Roll in flour, dip in beaten egg, roll again in flour. Brown in butter.

Stuffed Mushrooms

Orya Craven, Chef, La Fonda Hotel, Santa Fe, New Mexico

. . . .

24 fresh, large mushrooms
3 slices bread
1 lb. ground beef
$^1/_4$ cup chicken stock
$^1/_4$ cup Burgundy wine
1 small onion, finely chopped
and sautéed in butter

Wash mushrooms in salt water and drain. Cut off stems and chop them. Soak bread in chicken stock and squeeze out excess liquid. Mix chopped mushroom stems, beef, onion, egg, and bread. Season to taste with salt and pepper. Stuff mixture into mushroom caps. Bake in 350-degree oven until meat is done. Baste with Burgundy wine. This recipe can be used as a main course or appetizer. Crabmeat or chopped shrimp can be used in place of the beef.

Buttered Fresh Asparagus

Nelle Smith, Test Kitchen Supervisor

. . . .

Asparagus
Butter
Browned bread crumbs

Cut off hard end of asparagus (this may be used for soup). Wash asparagus, remove scales, keep in cold salted water until ready to cook. Lay stalks of asparagus flat in shallow pan, cover with boiling salted water, and allow to cook until tender (20 to 25 minutes). Drain off water (little should be left), then sprinkle with browned bread crumbs and melted butter.

Frijoles Refritos, La Fonda

Konrad Allgaier, Chef, La Fonda, La Fonda Hotel, Santa Fe, New Mexico

. . . .

2 cups pinto beans
4 slices bacon, diced
2 small cloves garlic, crushed
1 teaspoon salt
1 teaspoon finely chopped onion
$1/4$ teaspoon finely chopped
Chili pepper
Grated Parmesan cheese

Wash beans and soak over night in cold water to cover. Add bacon, cover, heat to boiling, and simmer for four hours. Drain and cool. Add garlic, onion, chili pepper, and salt; mix well, mashing slightly with a fork. Cook in shallow fat as for hashed brown potatoes. Serve with grated Parmesan cheese sprinkled over the top. Serves six.

Fresh Mushrooms Sauté

Mushrooms
Butter
Toast

Take a lump of fresh butter and simmer it to a golden brown, wash and peel the mushrooms, thoroughly dry, and fry until done. Serve on toast. No flour or wine or drawn butter should be used.

Candied Sweet Potatoes

Sweet Potatoes
Butter
Powdered Sugar

Boil in jackets, peel and cool; drop into drawn butter in an ovenproof frying pan and brown; draw off the butter and sprinkle with powdered sugar; place in a hot oven until glazed.

Potato Soufflé

George Burnickel, Chef, *California Limited*

4 large potatoes
1/2 cup milk
1 tablespoon butter
Salt and pepper
4 eggs, separated

Boil four good-sized mealy potatoes; pass them through a sieve. Scald in a saucepan half a teacup full of sweet milk and a tablespoonful of butter; add to the potatoes with a little salt and pepper and beat to a cream. Add, one at a time, the yolks of four eggs, beating thoroughly; put a small pinch of salt into the whites and beat them to a stiff froth, then add them to the mixture, beating as little as possible. Have ready a well-buttered baking dish, large enough to permit the soufflé to rise without running over; bake 20 minutes in a brisk oven, and serve at once in the same dish in which baked.

Stuffed Onions

Fred Guyer, Chef, *California Limited*

. . . .

Large white onions
2 cups bread crumbs
2 cups mushrooms

Parboil some large white onions in salt water for 20 minutes; drain and let cool. With a teaspoon or a large vegetable scoop take out the inner part of the onions. Add to this two handfuls of bread crumbs and two of mushrooms. Chop the whole fine, put in a saucepan with a ladleful of water. Fill onions and cook till onion is done.

Cauliflower Polonaise

. . . .

Cauliflower
Melted butter
Bread Crumbs
Lemon Juice

Pour over the cooked cauliflower a sauce of melted butter and lightly browned bread crumbs, seasoned with lemon juice.

Escalloped Eggplant

George Burnickel, Chef, *California Limited*

. . . .

2 large eggplants
Butter
Salt and pepper
Bread crumbs

Peel two large eggplants; boil until very tender. Drain, chop fine, and season to taste with butter, pepper, and salt. Put into an earthen pudding dish and cover the top with an inch layer of bread crumbs sprinkled with salt and dotted with bits of butter. Bake in a moderate oven until a rich brown.

Baked Tomatoes for Garnish

Dan Tachet, Chef, Castañeda, Las Vegas, New Mexico

. . . .

Tomatoes
Bread crumbs
Green onions
Cream sauce
Green pepper
Grated cheese
1 clove garlic

Dip some fresh tomatoes into boiling water one minute. Cut them in two crosswise; press lightly to get out some of the seeds, and peel them. Chop up some green onions, green peppers, a clove of garlic; mix with the same amount of fresh bread crumbs and fill up the cavities of the seeded tomatoes. Put cream sauce over each one. Sprinkle some grated cheese over them or cover with a thin slice of American cheese. Bake them and serve as a garnish.

Summer Squash

Dan Tachet, Chef, Castañeda, Las Vegas, New Mexico

. . . .

12 summer squash
4 peeled and cut-up tomatoes
4 oz. American cheese
3 onions
2 to 3 green peppers
1 clove garlic
Lard
Grated cheese

Remove the stems from the young squash; wash and slice them. Cut up some onions and green peppers; put them on the fire in a copper pot, with a little lard. When done, add one crushed clove of garlic, tomatoes, and the squash. Cook until tender. Take off the fire and add the cut-up cheese. Mix well and season. Put the mixture in a pan or a baker's platter and sprinkle with grated cheese. Put in an oven until a nice brown color.

Bell Pepper

(Ford Harvey Style)

. . . .

6 skinned bell peppers
(enough to make twelve orders)
2 or 3 onions
3 oz. butter or olive oil
1 bell pepper
1 tablespoon flour
1 crushed clove of garlic
3 or 4 eggplants
2 whole eggs
$^1/_2$ pint of milk
Handful of fresh bread crumbs
Grated cheese

Remove the skin from the peppers by dipping them into hot grease. Peel the eggplant and cut in dice a quarter of an inch thick. Cut the peppers in two lengthwise, remove the fleshy part adhering to the seeds, chop it and add to the eggplant. Cut the onions and single bell pepper fine; put on the fire with oil or butter and let cook for ten minutes. Add the crumbs, garlic, eggplant, and a little salt, and stir frequently until done. Add the flour; mix well; pour in the milk; let come to a boil and keep stirring. Add the eggs and a little chopped parsley. Mix well, season if necessary, and remove from the fire. Stuff the bell peppers with this mixture. Sprinkle with grated cheese; put a small lump of butter on each one, and leave them in a hot oven long enough to produce a nice golden brown color.

Duchess Potatoes

. . . .

6 medium-sized potatoes
$^1/_4$ cup butter
Pinch nutmeg
$^1/_8$ teaspoon white pepper
1 teaspoon salt
2 tablespoons milk
1 egg, lightly beaten
1 egg yolk, lightly beaten
1 egg beaten with 1 teaspoon cold water (glaze)

Boil the potatoes and allow to cool. Peel and mash the potatoes and measure four cups. Beat butter, nutmeg, pepper and salt, milk, egg, and egg yolk into the potatoes. Meanwhile, preheat boiler. Fill a pastry bag fitted with a large rosette tip with the potato mixture and press out onto a lightly greased baking sheet, forming 12 spiral cones about 2 $^1/_2$ inches in diameter. Or simply spoon potatoes into 12 mounds. Brush lightly with egg glaze. Broil five inches from heat three to five minutes until lightly browned, and serve. Serves six.

CHAPTER SIX

Montezuma and More

. . . .

In 1882, the Santa Fe Railroad opened a luxury hotel and spa in New Mexico Territory, at Montezuma Hot Springs near Las Vegas (Las Vegas means "The Meadows" in Spanish). A short branch line connected the resort with the main line at Las Vegas. This was generally considered to have been the first luxury resort in the Southwest, and it immediately attracted an international upscale clientele. Former presidents Ulysses Grant and Rutherford Hayes and their wives were numbered among its guests during its first few years, along with a string of European royalty. Plain old wealthy Americans also came, curious to see what the West was like.

And what *was* the West like? One way to put it might be, the elegance, sophistication, and gentility that visitors found at the Montezuma—which equaled any resort in America—did not prevail elsewhere in the territory. From the beginning, food service at the Montezuma was provided by Fred Harvey. From its opening day in 1882 onward, no apologies were needed for the standards of culinary fare and service. The opening banquet menu featured Blue Point oysters, mountain trout, spring lamb, and roast duck.

What is significant is that none of these menu items for the internationally renowned Montezuma was far from the normal fare at any of the Harvey Houses. In fact, in Las Vegas, there was also a Harvey House lunchroom at the railroad depot, where despite great differences in the atmosphere and clientele, Fred Harvey insisted that the food quality and selections be virtually the same. Indeed, terrapin, quail, sole, salmon, shrimp, and outstanding Kansas City steaks were no strangers to any Harvey House menu.

As time went on, Fred Harvey's interests included the company's own dairy and produce farms, a cattle ranch, and a central laundry. Even the Harvey House coffee

The magnificent Montezuma at Hot Springs near Las Vegas, New Mexico. One of the first resort hotels in the West, its facilities and popularity rivaled those of older European spas frequented by royalty. The Santa Fe owned, and Fred Harvey operated, the hotel from 1882 to 1902.

blend was adjusted for each locality, to compensate for differences in the taste of the local water. Fred Harvey coffee had a consistent taste across the continent. Where the local water was totally unusable, Harvey prevailed upon the Santa Fe to haul in tank cars full of spring water.

None of this exquisite attention to detail was lost on the Santa Fe publicity department, which consistently used the Harvey presence to distinguish its service from that of obviously inferior competitors. "Meals by Fred Harvey" became a well-used slogan. Nor was Harvey himself oblivious to the publicity to be gained by such generosity toward customers, or through his flamboyant quality control.

In his widening interests, Fred Harvey continued his practice of hiring outstanding chefs and paying them premium wages. He even recruited some of the finest chefs in Europe. Their contributions made the Harvey Houses and the Santa Fe resort hotels into what was described quite simply as "the best food service in the world."

Not only were the chefs outstanding individually, but they all shared recipes so that their ideas and skills were transferred throughout the Harvey system and refined

The Hotel Castañeda in Las Vegas, New Mexico, as it looked in 1905. In addition to forty-five guest rooms and dining facilities, the building contained a bakery, a commissary, regional offices, and other support facilities for Fred Harvey operations in the region. (Museum of New Mexico)

in this process of mutual contribution. Young American cooks received unsurpassed (if demanding) training at the hands of these masters, and if successful, they were promoted, most often to other locations.

Gradually, popular dishes became available throughout the system. At first, the Boss and his traveling assistants were the instruments of transfer and change, making sure that a dish was prepared in the same outstanding way at Albuquerque as it was at Topeka. In later years, the Fred Harvey Test Kitchens provided the means for circulating successful recipes from their place of origin to the entire system.

An 1888 menu has survived and is reproduced on page 5. As you read it, remember that it is not the Montezuma resort menu. This meal was generally available on the plains of Kansas, in a group of small towns. More important, it comes from no special occasion but from any typical day. Regrettably, the dinner price had gone up from 50 to 75 cents by then, and by 1928 it had skyrocketed to $1.75.

With the success of the Montezuma, the Santa Fe began to think about more such resorts in the Southwest. In 1898 came the opening of the Castañeda, also in Las Vegas, New Mexico, but at trackside. The new hotel housed a large bakery that supplied itself and Harvey Houses up and down the line. Las Vegas in fact became something of a center for Harvey activity, as local dairy farms and other suppliers were developed to equip the system.

The Castañeda also was home base for a $200,000 silver service, part or all of which was used there. When necessary, it was transported aboard an express railway car to whatever Harvey House needed it for a day or two to entertain a dignitary, or for other special occasions.

The ultimate special occasions at the Castañeda, beginning in 1899, were the annual reunions of the Rough Riders, complete with the then governor of New York, Theodore Roosevelt. Selection of the Castañeda for these events is easily explained: almost half of the Rough Riders were recruited for the Spanish-American War from New Mexico. The Castañeda remained a well-known hotel/resort until it was closed in 1948.

In 1899, the Mission-style Alvarado opened in Albuquerque; it became the largest and best known of the Santa Fe trackside hotels. It was Albuquerque's first luxury hotel, and its interior designs—Southwest Indian motifs by artist Mary Colter—achieved nationwide recognition. While it served as a resting place for travelers and visitors, being next to the railroad depot, the Alvarado also became a focus for local activities and a center for Indian art.

The Alvarado complex included the Indian Building, which became the focal point for the Harvey company's sales of Indian arts and crafts. At a time when few people were paying attention to Native Americans as artists, Ford Harvey and Minnie Harvey Huckel, Fred Harvey's son and daughter, saw the beauty and value of their work. They created the Fred Harvey Indian Department, which also reflected the interest of Harvey manager Herman Schweizer, who had begun to amass a collection of Navajo and other Indian creations. The Harvey company embarked on a system-wide program to promote and sell Indian-made blankets, jewelry, tapestries, baskets and other items. In so doing, they significantly increased the revenues of the Indian artists, and they helped swell public awareness of a culture that had been virtually ignored up to that time. The Alvarado was closed and torn down by the railroad in 1969.

The string of Santa Fe hotels reached from Kansas to California. In addition to the Castañeda and Alvarado, the first group included the Cardinas in Trinidad, Colorado, built in 1895 and closed in 1933. Five more hotels went up along the Santa Fe right of way at the turn of the century. The first two were the El Vaquero in Dodge City, Kansas, and the Gran Quivera in Clovis, New Mexico, both opened in 1900.

Three more lineside hotels opened in 1901: the Arcade in Newton, Kansas; the El Garces in Needles, California; and the El Otero in La Junta, Colorado. All five of these were closed in the late 1940s, as streamlined trains eliminated the desirability of stopovers en route except at the places most attractive to tourists.

During the time when these hotels and restaurants were opening, around the turn of the century, Fred Harvey's health was waning, and he died in 1901. His place at the head of the company was taken by his eldest son, Ford Harvey, who had been

The dining room of the El Vaquero Hotel in Dodge City, Kansas, was typical of Fred Harvey operations. Note the unusual arrangement of chairs. Harvey managers found that this arrangement—eight to a table, two per side—facilitated seating of traveling singles, couples, and foursomes at the same table. The tables' square shape did not impose intimacy upon the diners, but did allow conversation when desired.
(Santa Fe Collections, Kansas State Historical Society)

working in the firm for a few years at the time.

Though the company had lost its founder, Fred Harvey's image and spirit lived on to an extent not seen in many enterprises. Even a half century after his passing, the company carefully promoted the phrase "Meals by Fred Harvey" as its slogan. Ford Harvey arranged for the full, formal name of the company to be and remain just plain "Fred Harvey," without any further description such as "Inc.," "& Co.," or "Corp." While proper respect was accorded to the founder at the time of his death, the company continued to present itself as if Fred Harvey were still there.

In a sense, he *was* still there, because his sons Ford and Byron and their associates continued to follow the principles of service that they had been taught. The company remained very much a family business, with grandsons rising in the ranks through the 1950s.

An early example of the Indian curio shops installed by Fred Harvey in a number of larger stations and hotels. This one was in El Paso, Texas. The Harvey company insisted that the Native American craftsmen and women be treated fairly, and their goods achieved wide distribution. (Special Collections, University of Arizona Library)

Desserts

Peach Alexandria

Charles Zuellig, Chef, Alvarado Hotel, Albuquerque, New Mexico

. . . .

1/2 preserved peach
1 scoop vanilla ice cream
1/2 cup strawberry purée
3 tablespoons whipped cream

Place half of preserved peach on vanilla ice cream in iced supreme glass. Cover with strawberry purée and garnish with whipped cream. Serves one.

Peaches au Gratin

George Burnickel, Chef, *California Limited*

. . . .

Peaches
Sugar
Butter
2 teaspoons lemon juice
Bread crumbs
3 tablespoons drawn butter
3 tablespoons whipped cream

This dish can be made from either canned or fresh peaches; if the latter are used they must be cut into halves and stewed with plenty of sugar and a small quantity of water. Thickly butter a baking dish; drain the peaches from the syrup; lay them in a dish (cut side down) and strew over them plenty of grated bread crumbs. Mix with the syrup two teaspoonfuls of lemon juice and pour over the peaches; strew more bread crumbs over the top and baste them with a few table-spoonfuls of drawn butter. Put the dish in a hot oven and bake until lightly browned over the top. Serve with whipped cream.

Croquettes of Apples

Fred Guyer, Chef, *California Limited*

. . . .

12 large apples
8 oz. sugar
2 oz. butter
6 egg yolks
1 lemon rind
1/2 tablespoon potato starch
Pulverized crackers
Beaten egg
Bread crumbs
Powdered sugar

Peel and core 12 large apples; slice and put in a saucepan with two ounces of butter, the rind of a lemon, and eight ounces of sugar. Stir on the fire and reduce till very thick. Add the yolks of six eggs and 1/2 tablespoonful of potato starch. Mix well, stir a few minutes longer, rub through a sieve, spread on a buttered dishpan, and cool thoroughly. Turn on a table strewn with pulverized crackers; divide and shape. Dip in beaten egg, roll in bread crumbs, smooth nicely and fry brown, in plenty of hot fat. Drain on a cloth and roll in powdered sugar.

Maple Melange

Fred Wendell, Inspector

. . . .

1 cup maple syrup
1 cup steamed figs
1/2 box granulated gelatin
Powdered sugar
1 teaspoon vanilla
1 pint heavy cream
Whipped cream
Macaroon crumbs

To one cupful of maple syrup add 1/2 box of granulated gelatin which has been soaked in 1/2 cupful of cold water and dissolved by placing the cup in hot water. Flavor with one teaspoonful of vanilla. Cut into very small pieces one cupful of steamed figs. Dust with powdered sugar and add to the syrup. When it is sufficiently stiff, fold in one pint of whipped cream and place on ice until firm enough to form into croquettes. Pack in a freezer for four hours, then cover each croquette with macaroon crumbs, which have been rolled fine, and serve with whipped cream.

Strawberry Shortcake with Biscuit Dough

à la Dearborn Street Station

. . . .

4 boxes crushed berries
(reserving a few whole)
1 lb. flour
¹/₄ lb. granulated sugar
1 oz. baking powder
3 oz. butter
1 quart milk
Whipped cream

Mix biscuit ingredients. Bake, then split in two, and spread with whipped cream and berries between the two layers. Then place together and decorate heavily with whipped cream, with a few berries on top.

Chocolate Puffs

George Burnickel, Chef, *California Limited*

. . . .

1 cup flour
1 oz. melted chocolate
1 cup water
3 eggs
¹/₂ cup butter
Strawberry preserves
Whipped cream

Boil together one cupful of flour, one cupful of water, and half a cupful of butter. Remove from the fire and beat in an ounce of melted chocolate and three eggs (one at a time). Bake in a gem pan, and when done cut off the top and put into each cake a teaspoonful of strawberry preserves. Cover with whipped cream, sweetened and flavored.

Cheese Cake

Henry C. Ibsch, Head Baker, Los Angeles Union Station, California

. . . .

2 cups fine graham cracker
crumbs (25 crackers)
1 1/2 cups sugar
1/2 cup melted butter
4 eggs
2 tablespoons all-purpose flour
2 tablespoons cornstarch
1/8 teaspoon salt
2 teaspoons grated lemon peel
1 1/2 teaspoons lemon juice
1 teaspoon vanilla
1 cup cream
1 1/2 lbs. dry, small curd
cottage cheese

Mix crumbs with 1/2 cup sugar and the melted butter; reserve 3/4 cup crumbs for topping. Press remaining crumbs into a nine-inch spring form pan, lining bottom and sides. Build up sides to 1 3/4 inch height. Beat eggs with remaining one cup sugar until light; add flour, cornstarch, salt, lemon peel, lemon juice, vanilla, cream, and cheese. Beat thoroughly. Pour into crumb-lined pan; sprinkle with remaining crumbs. Bake in a moderate oven (350 degrees) one hour. Cool in pan. Remove from pan.

1 egg white, beaten stiff
2 tablespoons sugar
1/2 cup sour cream

Topping

Top with a mixture made by combining beaten egg white, sugar, and sour cream.

Lemon Cream Pie

Crust

1 cup sifted pastry flour
1/3 cup of part lard and butter
1 1/2 teaspoon salt
1/4 teaspoon baking powder
2 to 3 tablespoons cold water

Sift dry ingredients together, rub lard and butter into flour until it crumbles, then stir water in lightly with a fork (only enough water is needed to hold the flour together). As soon as that is accomplished it must be like a ball of putty when handled, requiring very little flour when rolling out. Line a deep pie plate with a thin sheet of the crust, letting it project above the rim of the plate, and flute the upstanding edge by pressing into scallops between thumbs and forefingers of both hands.

Filling

1 1/2 cups water
4 tablespoons lemon juice
1 cup sugar
3 egg yolks
1/3 cup cornstarch
(carefully measured)
Grated rind of 1 lemon

Moisten the cornstarch with about 1/4 cupful of the water, then add the lemon juice, grated rind, and half the sugar to the remaining water and bring to boiling point. Add to this the dissolved cornstarch and let boil until clear, about five minutes. Beat the yolks and the last half of the sugar until smooth; stir into the boiling starch and remove from fire at once. (This insures a firmer pie than if yolk is boiled before baking.) Now fill the prepared crust and bake until the custard is well set and the crust is golden brown. When done, let it cool before adding the meringue, or it will steam and spoil the delicate texture.

3 egg whites
1/2 teaspoon cream of tartar
6 level tablespoons granulated sugar
Lemon extract

Meringue

Whip whites with egg beater until they froth, then add the cream of tartar and whip until stiff. Now add the sugar, two tablespoonfuls at a time, beating one minute each time. At the last add the lemon extract and beat two minutes, then pile evenly on top of the pie (using part of the meringue to run in waves around the edge through a paper funnel). Set in moderately hot oven until a light golden brown. Let it remain in a warm place until cold or it will fall.

Quick (or Ersatz) Dobos Torte

R. T. Hillyard, Superintendent of Dining Cars

. . . .

1 (10 oz.) rectangular pound cake
2/3 cup whipping cream
1 1/3 package (1 1/3 cups)
semi-sweet chocolate bits
2 packages (1/4 lb.) German
sweet chocolate

Trim crusts from cake. Cut cake in half lengthwise. Slice each half into eight slices, lengthwise and parallel with top. Melt the chocolate bits over hot water, remove from hot water, and let cool while whipping the cream, stiff but not dry. Fold chocolate into whipped cream. Spread between layers of each half cake. Melt German chocolate over warm water. Pour over top and sides of cake to make a thin coating. Chill cake until firm. Slice and serve. Yield: two cakes, each 4 3/4" x 2" x 2 1/2" or 16 servings, 5/8 inch thick.

Royal Chocolate Layer Cake

Hermann Wendel, Chef, Kent County Airport, Michigan

· ·

6 egg yolks
6 egg whites
2 tablespoons sugar
2 tablespoons flour
1 tablespoon vanilla
1/4 teaspoon salt
2 tablespoons water
1/2 teaspoon baking powder

Whip egg yolks with sugar and water on medium mixer setting until light and fluffy. Whip egg whites and vanilla until stiff and fold into egg yolk mixture. Gently fold in flour, salt, and baking powder, which have been sifted together. Bake in 10-inch diameter, three-inch deep pan at 375 degrees, for approximately 35 minutes.

1 pint milk
1 tablespoon cornstarch
3 oz. bittersweet chocolate, melted
6 egg yolks
3 1/4 tablespoons sugar
16 oz. unsalted butter
1/2 teaspoon lemon extract
1/2 teaspoon arrack
1 tablespoon vanilla
1 cup crushed raspberries

Filling

Bring milk and sugar to a boil; add two tablespoons cold milk to cornstarch, add to boiling milk, and cook for three minutes. Remove from heat, add egg yolks and melted chocolate; cool, stirring occasionally. Whip butter until fluffy; add extracts; blend chocolate pudding mixture into butter and extracts. Cut cake into three layers and put together with chocolate filling and one cup crushed raspberries. First spread crushed raspberries on top of layer, then chocolate mixture. Decorate top of cake with chocolate filling put through a pastry tube, and finish top and sides with two cups of chocolate decorettes.

Lemon Chiffon Cheese Cake Dessert

Nelle Smith, Test Kitchen Supervisor

. . . .

¹/2 cup lemon Jell-O
1 cup boiling water
¹/2 lb. cream cheese
¹/2 teaspoon vanilla
1 teaspoon lemon juice
Graham cracker crust
2 tablespoons sugar
1 can Milnot, chilled
(or Dream Whip)

Filling

Combine Jell-O and boiling water; chill, but do not allow to jell. Combine cream cheese, sugar, and vanilla, whip until very soft, then stir into liquid Jell-O. Whip Milnot until stiff. Combine all ingredients. Pour into deep pie pan which has been lined with graham cracker crust and chill.

¹/2 cup sugar
¹/2 cup melted butter
1 ¹/2 cups graham cracker crumbs

Crust

Mix all ingredients together. Line pie tin using back of spoon to press the bottom and sides firmly. Bake in 350-degree oven for five minutes. Place in refrigerator and chill before filling.

Banana Pie

. . . .

Bananas
Allspice or ginger
Sugar
Acid syrup
Butter
Lemon or orange juice

Peel and slice the bananas thin; add sugar, a little butter, some spice (allspice or a dash of ginger), a little acid syrup, and lemon or orange juice. Bake with full cover (top crust) or put on a meringue when done. Another way is to make a syrup with ¹/2 pint of water and vinegar, one pound of sugar, and some allspice, and season the bananas with the syrup.

113

Empanadas with Vanilla Sauce

Konrad Allgaier, Chef, La Fonda Hotel, Santa Fe, New Mexico

. . . .

1 $1/2$ cups finely chopped
cooked beef
1 $1/2$ teaspoons crushed oregano
$1/4$ cup sugar
2 oz. suet, chopped fine
1 1-lb. jar mincemeat
1 tablespoon grated lemon peel
1 recipe plain pastry
(using 2 cups flour)

Combine beef, mincemeat, suet, oregano, sugar, and lemon peel. Roll pastry and cut in six-inch circles. Place $1/3$ cup filling on each pastry circle, fold in half, and flute edge. Prick to allow steam to escape. Fry in deep hot fat. Serve with hot vanilla sauce. Yield: 12 turnovers.

$3/4$ cup butter
3 tablespoons cornstarch
1 $1/2$ cups sugar
3 cups boiling water
3 teaspoons vanilla

Vanilla Sauce

Melt butter; blend in cornstarch and sugar. Add boiling water, stirring constantly, and cook until thickened. Add vanilla just before serving.

7-Up with Sherbet

Nelle Smith, Test Kitchen Supervisor

. . . .

7-Up
Orange or pineapple sherbet

Pour chilled 7-Up into juice glass; fill to $1/2$ inch of rim. Place orange or pineapple sherbet in 7-Up and serve.

Grand Canyon Strawberry Surprise

George Davis, Cafeteria Sous Chef

. . . .

1 pint fresh strawberries cut in half
4 tablespoons Jamaica Rum
3/4 cup strained honey
Rind of one orange cut in strips
4 tablespoons lemon juice

Marinate strawberries in rum one hour. Combine honey, lemon juice, and orange peel; bring to a boil. Remove peel; combine honey mixture and strawberries. Serve over ice cream, immediately. Remainder can be refrigerated; reheat in double boiler. Makes 2 1/4 cups or about eight servings.

Brandy Flip Pie

Adolphe Achenbach, Chef, Chicago Union Station, Illinois

. . . .

1 tablespoon (1 envelope) unflavored gelatin
1/4 cup cold water
4 beaten egg yolks
1/2 cup sugar
1/2 cup milk, scalded
4 egg whites
1/2 teaspoon nutmeg
3 or 4 tablespoons brandy
1 baked 9-inch pastry shell
Whipped cream
Chocolate curls

Soften gelatin in cold water. Combine egg yolks, 1/4 cup sugar, and milk; cook in double boiler until mixture coats spoon. Remove from heat. Add gelatine and stir until dissolved. Chill until slightly thickened. Fold in egg whites, which have been beaten stiff with remaining sugar, nutmeg, and brandy. Pour into cooled, baked pastry shell. Chill until firm. Serve with whipped cream garnished with chocolate curls. Make chocolate curls by shaving slightly warmed bitter or semi-sweet chocolate with long blade of a potato peeler.

Date Sticks

Nelle Smith, Test Kitchen Supervisor

. . . .

2 eggs, separated

1 teaspoon baking powder

³/₄ cup sugar

1 cup dates, cut fine

1 cup nuts, cut fine

¹/₄ cup sifted flour

1 teaspoon vanilla

Separate eggs. Whip yolks till light. Stir in sugar; mix well. Mix flour, baking powder, nuts, and dates together; stir into egg mixture. Beat whites of eggs stiff; fold into mixture; mix well. Add vanilla. Place in greased and floured 8" x 8" cake pan. Bake in 300-degree oven for 35 minutes.

Chocolate Clusters

Nelle Smith, Test Kitchen Supervisor

. . . .

1 pkg. chocolate pudding,
not instant

1 cup sugar

¹/₂ cup canned condensed milk

2 teaspoons vanilla

1 cup salted nuts or

1 ¹/₂ cups raisins

Over medium fire, cook pudding mix, sugar, and milk until it comes to a rolling boil. Lower heat and cook three minutes. Remove from fire, beat vigorously, stir in vanilla. Stir in either nuts or raisins (a matter of choice). Beat until the candy starts to thicken. Drop from teaspoon on to oiled paper. Yield 12 to 16 clusters.

Apple Sauce Cake

Nelle Smith, Test Kitchen Supervisor

. . . .

1 teaspoon cocoa
1 cup unsweetened applesauce
^{1}/2 cup shortening or butter
1 cup raisins
1 cup brown sugar
1 teaspoon baking soda
1 egg
^{1}/2 teaspoon cinnamon
1 ^{1}/2 cup sifted flour
^{1}/2 teaspoon cloves
Dash nutmeg

Cream cocoa, butter, and sugar. Stir in whole egg; mix well. Alternately add flour and apple sauce. Stir in raisins, soda, and spices. Place in greased and floured pan 3" x 5" x 9". Bake in 250-degree oven for one hour.

Sopaipillas

La Fonda Hotel, Santa Fe, New Mexico

. . . .

1 package active dry or
1 cake compressed yeast
^{1}/4 cup water
^{3}/4 cup milk, scalded
6 tablespoons sugar
2 tablespoons shortening
1 teaspoon salt
1 egg, beaten
3 cups all-purpose flour (approx.)

Soften active dry yeast in warm water (110 degrees) or compressed yeast in lukewarm water (85 degrees). Combine milk, sugar, shortening, and salt; cool to lukewarm. Add softened yeast and egg. Gradually stir in flour; mix to a smooth dough. Let rise until double in bulk, for about 1 ^{1}/2 hours. Roll on floured surface to a 12" x 12" square; cut in twenty-four strips, each 2" x 3". Fry in hot deep fat (350 degrees) about three minutes, turning once.

French Apple Pie with Nutmeg Sauce

Henry C. Ibsch, Head Baker, Los Angeles Union Station, California

· ·

8 cups sliced, pared, tart apples
¹/2 cup water
1 ¹/2 cups sugar
1 recipe plain pastry
1 cup graham cracker crumbs
¹/2 cup all-purpose flour
¹/2 cup sugar
¹/3 cup butter
Few drops vanilla

Cook apples in water until tender; add sugar and mix carefully to retain shape of apples. Arrange apples in pastry-lined pie pan. Combine graham cracker crumbs, flour, sugar, butter, and vanilla; mix until they resemble coarse crumbs. Sprinkle mixture over apples. Bake in hot oven (425 degrees) 10 minutes, then in moderate oven (350 degrees) 20 minutes. Serve with Nutmeg Sauce.

1 egg yolk
¹/2 cup sugar
1 cup milk
1 teaspoon nutmeg

Nutmeg Sauce

Beat together egg yolk, sugar, and milk. Heat to the boiling point; remove from heat and add nutmeg. Yield: 1 ¹/3 cups sauce.

Oatmeal Cookies

George Burnickel, Chef, *California Limited*

· ·

2 cups sugar
1 ¹/3 cups butter
4 eggs
4 cups sifted pastry flour
1 ¹/3 teaspoons baking soda
2 teaspoons cornstarch
4 cups rolled oats
2 cups shredded raisins
2 cups chopped nuts
2 teaspoons cinnamon

Stir sugar, butter, and eggs until light and creamy. Mix pastry flour, baking soda, cornstarch, and cinnamon. Stir into the butter, sugar and eggs; then add rolled oats (not cooked), shredded raisins and chopped nuts. Mix well; drop into tins and bake in a slow oven.

Scrambled Fruit Pie

. . . .

1 cup flour
1/4 cup sugar
1/2 cup margarine

Crust

Mix well and pat into eight-inch square pan. Bake in moderate oven (350 degrees) for about 20 minutes until light brown.

1 cup brown sugar
2 eggs
2 tablespoons flour
2/3 teaspoon baking powder
1 teaspoon vanilla
Pinch salt
1/2 cup dried coconut
Whipped cream or ice cream (optional)
1/2 cup chopped nuts (not peanuts)
1/2 cup fruit cake mixture
(or any dried fruit
cut into small pieces)

Filling

Mix all together, spread on the finished crust, and bake 15 minutes. It's almost painting the lily, but for gala effect you might top with whipped cream or balls of ice cream.

Soft White Frosting

Nelle Smith, Test Kitchen Supervisor

. . . .

1 *1/2* cups sugar
1/2 teaspoon cream of tartar
3/4 cup water
3 egg whites, stiffly beaten
1 teaspoon vanilla
1 pkg. shredded coconut

Boil sugar, water, and cream of tartar to form soft base in cold water. Pour into stiffly beaten egg white, whipping continuously. Add vanilla, whip until stiff enough to spread over cake. Sprinkle coconut over frosting while still sticky.

Cranberry Mold

Nelle Smith, Test Kitchen Supervisor

. . . .

1 cup crushed and drained pineapple
(reserve juice)
2 pkg. cherry Jell-O
1 cup sugar
1 1/2 cup boiling water
Cottage cheese
1 tablespoon fresh lemon juice
3/4 cup chopped walnuts
1 1/2 cup ground raw cranberries
1 cup chopped celery
1 cup ground whole orange
(remove seeds)
Green maraschino cherries

Dissolve Jell-O and sugar in hot water; add pineapple syrup and lemon juice. Chill until the mixture is partially set. Add all the other ingredients. Pour into any shape mold or individual molds. Fill center with cottage cheese, and garnish with green maraschino cherries. Serves 10 to 12 persons.

Hot Strawberry Sundae

Joe Maciel, Westport Room Manager, Kansas City Union Station, Missouri

. . . .

1 pint strawberries, cut in half
4 tablespoons Jamaica Rum
3/4 cup strained honey
4 tablespoons lemon juice
Rind of 1 orange, cut in strips
Ice cream

Marinate strawberries in rum for one hour. Bring honey, lemon juice, and orange peel to a boil; remove orange rind and combine flavored honey with strawberries. Serve over ice cream immediately. Yield: about 2 1/4 cups.

About 1,300 miles and forty years separate this recipe from the one at the top of page 115. We include them both as an example of Fred Harvey consistency despite large differences in time and space.

Chestnut Pudding

Johan Mayr, Chef, Palmolive Building, Chicago, Illinois

. . . .

2 lbs. chestnuts
1/2 stick of cinnamon
2 1/2 oz. cornstarch
1/8 quart cream
8 oz. butter
5 oz. sugar
6 eggs
Milk
Burgundy or Punch Sauce

Boil the chestnuts just enough to peel easily. Cook chestnuts in milk, barely enough to cover, and a half stick of cinnamon. When nice and done, take cinnamon stick out and press chestnuts through a fine sieve. Mix separately 1/8 quart of cream with one ounce butter and 2 1/2 ounces cornstarch. Mix to a smooth paste and heat. Add the chestnut purée; make a nice mixture; and chill. Whip the remaining seven ounces of butter with five ounces of sugar and two whole eggs and four egg yolks. (Save the whites for later use.) A few almonds, finely chopped or finely ground, add to the flavor. When chestnut mixture is well whipped, blend in the four egg whites whipped stiff. Now put the pudding into a form and cook over boiling water, as is done in making any pudding. Because of the chestnuts, this pudding will take a little longer in cooking. When cold, tip the pudding out of the form. Serve with Burgundy (or a sweet red wine) sauce or Punch Sauce.

Cream Cheese Frosting

Nelle Smith, Test Kitchen Supervisor

. . . .

3 oz. cream cheese
1 tablespoon lemon juice
1 teaspoon lemon rind
2 1/2 cups confectioners sugar, sifted

Blend cream cheese, juice, and rind; add sugar gradually. Mix well.

CHAPTER SEVEN

The Resort Hotels

· ·

With the exception of the Montezuma, the first Santa Fe hotels were built to accommodate passengers and train crews, as close adjuncts to the railroad service. The Montezuma experience gave Santa Fe managers an insight into a new market: tourism. The next wave of resort hotels that Fred Harvey operated would thus be designed as destinations in themselves, rather than simply stops along the way.

In 1903, the Santa Fe shifted its primary tourist focus westward to the Grand Canyon. A branch line from Williams and Anita, Arizona, to the canyon had opened in 1901. The railroad built the hundred-room El Tovar hotel adjacent to the canyon rim as a resort hotel. Ultimately a cluster of buildings and a community grew up around El Tovar, which was fully opened by 1905. The Montezuma was closed in 1901, and the Fred Harvey senior staff moved almost as a unit to start up the new El Tovar.

The Grand Canyon's remote location, and the primitive state of photographic and aviation development, combined to make the canyon almost unknown in America until the Santa Fe began to publicize it. In fact, for most Americans the first view of the canyon was a color lithograph that the railroad commissioned and then distributed nationwide to schools and other institutions.

But a remote location did not in any way lower the standards and amenities of service provided. The Harvey organization put a first-class team of chefs in place and gradually built up a series of mule and walking tours and other tourist attractions. The El Tovar guest list came to include many notable names from America and abroad, including presidents and royalty coming to view the scenic wonders amid elegant surroundings.

*A more or less typical day at the El Tovar Hotel, on the rim of the Grand Canyon,
when the century was young. The Santa Fe and Fred Harvey combined to make this one
of the premier vacation destinations in the United States.*

Part of the canyon complex was the Hopi House Indian Museum, exhibiting that Native American tribe's heritage. Mary Colter, now the Fred Harvey company's resident architect, displayed her knack for vivid authenticity in this and other resort hotels built by the Santa Fe and operated by Fred Harvey.

In 1919, the Grand Canyon became a national park. In 1954, the Santa Fe sold its land and buildings to the U.S. Government, and the Fred Harvey company became the concessionaire for the canyon hotels and facilities.

The Grand Canyon complex was only one of a series of Santa Fe resort locations built in the early part of this century. Two more elegant hotels rose up in Arizona and two in Kansas; these were built on-line as comfortable stopovers. In Arizona, the Fray Marcos in Williams and the Escalante in Ash Fork both opened in 1905. In Kansas, the Bisonte in Hutchinson opened in 1906, and the Sequoyah opened in Syracuse in 1908.

Tourism at the Grand Canyon was and is a substantial contributor to Arizona's economy. The group of visitors about to board the Fred Harvey bus and touring cars at El Tovar in the late 1920s will be no less fascinated by the majestic scenery than are tourists today. (Museum of Northern Arizona)

Not all of these hotels were Mission- or Pueblo-style buildings. The Bisonte in particular was built in the Tudor mode, with a charm totally different from the southwestern ambience prevalent elsewhere. Ford Harvey made sure, however, that the service level did not vary from the excellent example set by his father until the hotels were closed in the 1940s.

One of the largest Santa Fe–Harvey facilities, Casa del Desierto (House of the Desert), opened in Barstow, California, in 1910. The hotel complex included an ice cream plant that supplied Harvey Houses in Arizona and California. Casa del Desierto closed in 1959, but its restoration in the 1990s is a source of considerable municipal pride.

By contrast, the other hotel to open in 1910, El Ortiz in Lamy, New Mexico, was the smallest of the Santa Fe–Harvey hotels. Though containing only about a dozen rooms, El Ortiz was an architectural gem inside and out, favored by many famous

An Indian Detour excursion is about to begin here at Lamy, New Mexico, in 1930. Two drivers (wearing ten-gallon Stetsons) are awaiting the couriers and remaining passengers. Lamy is the stop on the Santa Fe Railway main line closest to the city of Santa Fe. (Museum of New Mexico)

people precisely because of its small size and intimate atmosphere. El Ortiz closed in 1938.

The El Navajo Hotel in Gallup, New Mexico, another main Santa Fe–Harvey hotel, was dedicated to Native American artistry. Designed by Mary Colter, it bore Navajo sand paintings on the walls, among other artwork throughout. The paintings were sacred images, but Fred Harvey's reputation for honesty and fairness was such that the Navajo allowed Mary Colter to use the display. In fact, the El Navajo paintings received ritual blessing from tribal medicine men during a ceremony as the hotel opened in 1923.

La Fonda Hotel in Santa Fe, New Mexico, survived as a railroad operation until 1968. This is how it looked in 1950. (Foster Collection)

In the 1920s, the Inter-tribal Indian Ceremonials were centered around El Navajo. It was one of the few times when Harvey Girls wore a uniform other than their basic black and white, donning instead a specially designed, festive blouse-skirt combination. For Harvey employees, El Navajo became a coveted assignment, and its team was made up of experienced senior staff. For that reason, Gallup and El Navajo became a training ground for new Harvey Girls, as Headquarters knew they would be well taught there. El Navajo closed in 1957.

In 1929, the Santa Fe opened the rebuilt La Fonda hotel in Santa Fe, New Mexico, at the end of the old Santa Fe Trail. An inn had been on the site since the early 1600s,

La Fonda accommodations reflected a southwestern charm, just as Mary Colter intended. These photos of a living room and bedroom were taken in 1950 to record how the "old section" of the hotel looked before remodeling. (Foster collection)

and the railroad acquired the historic but bankrupt hotel in 1926. Mary Colter transformed the old hotel into a 156-room Harvey House, opening three years later. The motif here was Mexican, and the La Fonda Harvey House drew critical acclaim from all over.

La Fonda was also the headquarters for the famous Indian Detours, Fred Harvey's automobile touring service operated in New Mexico between 1926 and 1931. The Indian Detours were just that: first-class side trips through stunning southwestern scenery in large touring cars or small buses, depending on the route. Choosing this itinerary, a Santa Fe passenger could break the long train ride with a tour of New Mexico's culture and scenery. Each trip was run by two Harvey employees, a driver and a courier.

The Indian Detour crews were handpicked and well paid. Drivers were male and wore uniforms similar to the attire of western movie heroes. The couriers were articulate female college graduates who were knowledgeable about the Southwest (Harvey training filled in the gaps). Similar Detour operations were set up in Colorado and Arizona.

The longest New Mexico Indian Detour involved leaving the train at Las Vegas, touring for three or four days, including a stop at Santa Fe, and rejoining the railroad at Albuquerque. That trip could, of course, be made in either direction.

With the depression reducing the number of people willing to take such trips, the service was sold to local interests in 1931. Some of the Detour routes continued to operate until World War II. The Santa Fe likewise sold La Fonda in 1968, and operation continued under different owners.

The last of the Santa Fe–Harvey grand hotels to open was La Posada (The Resting Place) at Winslow, Arizona. In fact, so close did the depression fall upon the heels of its opening that the railroad came to lament the million-dollar expenditure very quickly. Mary Colter's final architectural masterpiece, La Posada was designed as a Spanish ranch house, with rare furnishings contributing to a general atmosphere of Hispanic elegance. Many travelers abruptly changed plans during a meal stop there, so they could stay over for a day or two. La Posada's seventy guest rooms were converted to railroad offices in 1957.

The Santa Fe–Harvey hotels offered a consistently high level of accommodations that made them vacation attractions in themselves. The railroad promoted this resort/tourist business extensively, operating as more than just a hauler of people and goods. Every traveler had his or her favorite hotel. The service policy was consistent, but each hotel had its own decor, flavor, and ambience, from the intimate El Ortiz to the bustling Alvarado to the spectacular El Tovar.

Travel on railroads hit its peak in the 1920s, falling off during the depression of the 1930s. World War II caused a significant upward surge in traffic, but most of that traffic was military related. After the war, many people turned to private automobiles for family travel. We should note that the segment of fabled U.S. Route 66 between Amarillo, Texas, and San Bernardino, California, paralleled the Santa Fe main line, which had preceded the highway. An increasing percentage of Santa Fe–Harvey hotel guests were arriving by automobile, but the total number of guests was gradually decreasing.

By the mid-1950s, more people were traveling by air. Introduction of jet aircraft in 1957 meant that the only force keeping rail passenger trains going was regulatory. The Interstate Commerce Commission would not allow abandonment of passenger train service, no matter how unprofitable.

Rail travel through spectacular scenery, augmented by good food and superior service, has now been replaced by jet aircraft and interstate highways, which allow a traveler to go from coast to coast without seeing anything, except plastic trays containing plastic food.

Train travel and the Santa Fe–Harvey hotels comprised a way of life now gone, and those who remember it lament its passing.

Breads & Muffins

Blueberry Muffins La Posada

Guy Falconer, Baker, La Posada, Winslow, Arizona

. . . .

2/3 cup sugar
1/3 cup shortening
4 teaspoons baking powder
2 eggs, beaten
2 cups sifted all-purpose flour
1/2 teaspoon salt
1 cup frozen blueberries, thawed
2/3 cup milk

Cream together sugar and shortening. Add eggs; mix well. Sift together flour, baking powder, and salt. Add alternately with milk to creamed mixture. Blend in blueberries. Fill greased muffin pans half full and bake in moderately hot oven (400 degrees) 15 minutes. Yields 1 1/2 dozen muffins.

Griddle Muffins

Nelle Smith, Test Kitchen Supervisor

. . . .

Corn muffin mix
Jam
Butter
Bacon (optional)

Use directions on package of corn muffin mix. Drop rounded tablespoons of mixture on greased griddle. Brown on both sides; split; serve with jam and butter. Chopped bacon is very good added to this mixture.

Corn Bread

1 lb. corn meal and flour
1/2 lb. sugar
2 oz. baking powder
1 teaspoon salt
3 eggs
2 oz. melted shortening
1 1/2 pint milk

Sift together corn meal, flour, sugar, baking powder and salt. Mix three eggs with 1 1/2 pints of milk and two ounces melted fat. Stir this into the sifted ingredients, pour it at once into a well-greased pan about an inch deep, and bake in a 400-degree oven for half an hour.

Corn Meal Mush

1 quart yellow corn meal
1 tablespoon butter
4 pints water
1 tablespoon salt

Add a pint of cold water to a quart of fresh yellow corn meal and mix well. Bring three pints of water, a level tablespoonful of salt, and as much butter to a boil, add the corn meal mixture, stir smooth, and let boil slowly for an hour and a half. This cereal is served with either milk or cream and brown or white sugar, honey, syrup, fruit juice, or melted butter. For fried mush pour the cooked mixture in a wet mold to cool and stiffen. Then cut it into suitable slices and fry.

Baked Mush

Corn meal mush
Butter

For baked mush boil only half as long as for regular corn meal mush, pour it into a low buttered fire proof dish or pan, brush the top with butter, and bake for about two hours in a moderately hot oven (375 degrees) so the top acquires an even brown crust. Serve hot with cream, sweetening, etc., or a tasty cheese.

Corn Pone

1 quart milk

1 teaspoon salt

24 oz. corn meal

2 oz. sugar

3 oz. shortening

1 or 2 eggs (optional)

Pour one quart of hot milk over 24 oz. of corn meal, stir in three ounces of good shortening, and then let the mass stand in a cool place over night. Next morning mix in a teaspoon of salt and two ounces of sugar and drop the mixture by spoonsful on a greased baking sheet. Bake at once for about 25 minutes in a 400-degree oven. Using an egg or two in the mixture is optional.

Corn Meal Croquettes

1 quart cooked corn meal mush

2 eggs

1 heaping tablespoon butter

Flour

$^1/_2$ teaspoon salt

Fat for frying

Shrimp or lobster sauce

Tomato sauce

To a quart of cooked and cooled corn meal mush add a heaping tablespoonful of butter, and a half teaspoonful of salt and two eggs. Mix well. When stiff, break out a tablespoonful at a time, roll on a floured board, and form into desired shapes such as two- to three-inch-long rolls, cones, or balls. Place on a suitable dish in the refrigerator to stiffen. Fry in deep grease, drain well, and serve attractively on folded napkin with a tasty shrimp or lobster sauce, a rich tomato sauce, or another suitable accompaniment.

Polenta

. . . .

1 quart milk
Salt
Corn meal
Butter
1 heaping tablespoon
grated Parmesan cheese

This is baked mush, made in this country with corn meal. Bring a quart of milk to a boil and sift in slowly just enough corn meal to make a thick porridge. Stir continually and when nice and smooth, mix in a heaping tablespoonful of grated Parmesan cheese and salt lightly. Pour the mixture in a buttered mold and bake for 20-30 minutes. Polenta can also be served differently by making the mixture same as for mush. Pour it in wet molds and let harden. Then cut it in small blocks, arrange them in a buttered baking dish or pan and sprinkle grated Parmesan cheese thickly between the layers and on top, then bake to a nice light brown color and serve hot.

CHAPTER EIGHT

Restaurants on Wheels

. . . .

We noted earlier that the first American long-distance trains provided for passenger meals at trackside stops, coincident with stops necessary to fill up the locomotive's tender with water. As locomotives and tenders became larger and more efficient, the need for such stops decreased. The desire to improve service by reducing train travel time led to the development of diner cars, rolling restaurants that permitted meals to be served without stopping the train. A relatively early development, the first railroad dining cars to be operated in America for more than a one-shot special occasion were run on the Pennsylvania and the Baltimore and Ohio railroads in the 1860s, even before the first transcontinental railroad was completed in 1869. By the mid–1880s "diners" were common on the railroads operating out of Chicago, and brought a welcome relief from bad trackside food.

Indeed, the diners were favored everywhere except on the Santa Fe, where the Harvey Houses were, by now, legendary. But even on the Santa Fe between Kansas City and Chicago, east of Fred Harvey territory, dining cars were in operation beginning in 1888. In 1892, the railroad introduced a new and elegant train, the *California Limited*, and its consist included operation of dining cars west of Kansas City, bypassing the Harvey Houses. Fred Harvey sued the railroad to squelch this threat to his business. Negotiations followed, and Fred Harvey wound up operating the Santa Fe's dining cars.

While the use of diners became widespread across the United States, they were never a source of profit to the railroad. The economics of dining-car operation are such that there is no way an operator can avoid losing money on this service. The capital investment to build a complex rail vehicle with a full kitchen, for what is essentially a 30- or 36-seat restaurant, is far more than what can be recovered. The costs of labor are also high; as many as four cooks and seven stewards are required

The California Limited

No. 5. THROUGH DINING CAR.

Built expressly for this service; wide vestibuled and electric lighted; provided with electric fans, and a device in the ceiling of kitchen which removes odor of cooking. The best railway meal service in the world.

No. 6. BUFFET-SMOKING CAR, FROM CHICAGO TO LOS ANGELES; WITH DUPLICATE CAR BARSTOW TO SAN FRANCISCO.

Baggage compartment in forward end. Buffet, barber shop, and smoking and reading room for gentlemen.

Diagrams of two cars used on the 1905 California Limited *illustrate the facilities and services to be found on a first-class train. On the Dining Car, the compact kitchen served rows of tables with four-and-two seating arrangements. The Buffet-Smoking Car (more often known as the Club Car) was, indeed, a male refuge. (Foster collection)*

Elegance on wheels! These turn-of-the-century passengers are seated in an ornate Santa Fe wooden dining car, about to enjoy a Fred Harvey meal. Look—could that be a senator or movie star at the next table? (Library of Congress)

for a three-day trip. And, unlike a stationary restaurant, the diner has no local trade to help cover the overhead costs.

Given the impossibility of turning a profit because of high fixed and variable costs, the Santa Fe and Fred Harvey pioneered the idea of deliberately losing a bit more money than the competing railroads, in order to provide the finest dining experience on wheels. This idea of attracting customers with good food—and making up for the high costs by increased ticket sales and good will—spread to many American railroads and led to the legends of good eating on the rails. The Fred Harvey organization was later to apply the concept of outstanding food and good service to air travel, for a mournfully short time.

The dining-car meals were, like the Harvey House fare, the best available for a discerning clientele. Because the railroad reimbursed Fred Harvey for losses incurred on the diners under a negotiated formula, the recipes and service on the Santa Fe trains were up to Fred Harvey standards. The only difference between the lineside restaurants and the dining cars was that the Harvey Girls were not employed in

Streamlined passenger trains introduced in the 1930s provided a brighter atmosphere than the old wooden cars. The Fred Harvey steward and waiter are about to prove that the service standard was still the best. There was no better way to travel in comfort; and, some say, there still is no better way. (Santa Fe Collections, Kansas State Historical Society)

dining-car service; all of the help was male.

It was necessary to staff the dining cars generously. The original *California Limited* cars were six seats (two tables) smaller than the cars that later became the standard. The normal diner configuration, as shown on page 138, calls for four-seat and two-seat table combinations throughout the car. The seating capacity dictated how many hungry passengers would be served per shift or seating. In some cases, with more than 300 people on board a train, as many as eight or ten seatings were required for one meal.

In later years, particularly on the *Chief* and *Super Chief* trains, dining cars were built in semipermanent two-car sets, one car containing forty-eight seats at sixteen tables and the other car containing a slightly larger kitchen and dormitory facilities for the train crew. This represented the maximum size for railway diners: 60 percent larger than the first *California Limited* cars.

The three or four cooks worked in an efficient (read "cramped") kitchen; it was only experience and adherence to procedures that avoided chaos. This work space was in sharp contrast to the relatively roomy Harvey House kitchens; yet, according to clientele response, the food was as good and as varied as that available in any good restaurant. The archives are full of complimentary letters from frequent travelers, many of whom arranged their travel schedules to be aboard the Santa Fe with its Fred

Top-quality ingredients remain the key to good cooking, at home or on wheels. Harvey crews loaded literally tons of meat, poultry, vegetables, and other ingredients aboard Santa Fe dining cars every day. Here, the Super Chief *is being provisioned for its journey. (Santa Fe Collections, Kansas State Historical Society)*

Harvey service.

On many trains, the dining cars were not the only source of food and drink. Light food and beverage service was provided as an alternate meal or between-meals snack on two other types of cars in the train. The first of these, literally, was the Club Car, usually coupled just behind the locomotive or the baggage and mail cars at the head of the train. It was the smoker, the male refuge, with leather easy chairs and a steward serving from a built-in bar and buffet. The liquor cabinet was locked or open, depending on the train's location. "Last call before the Kansas line" was a familiar cry when rolling into a dry county.

The diner usually occupied a position about midway in the train. At the rear, a Lounge Car offered comfortable chairs and light food for passengers of both sexes. Lounge Cars often had observation areas, many with open brass-railed platforms in the early days. These platforms bore many a candidate for political office, as well as everyday travelers with a penchant for open air. As trains became faster, the observation platforms were closed in but given large windows.

The Santa Fe and Fred Harvey led the way toward quality in food service and travel. In general, the food served on the railroads was ranked with the best available in America between 1900 and 1940. Much of Fred Harvey's reputation, and many of the recipes in this volume, came from these "Harvey Houses on Wheels."

To say that kitchens in dining cars were "compact" may be an understatement, especially with four men maneuvering in that narrow aisle simultaneously. But some of America's best food issued forth from these cramped quarters, every day. (Foster collection)

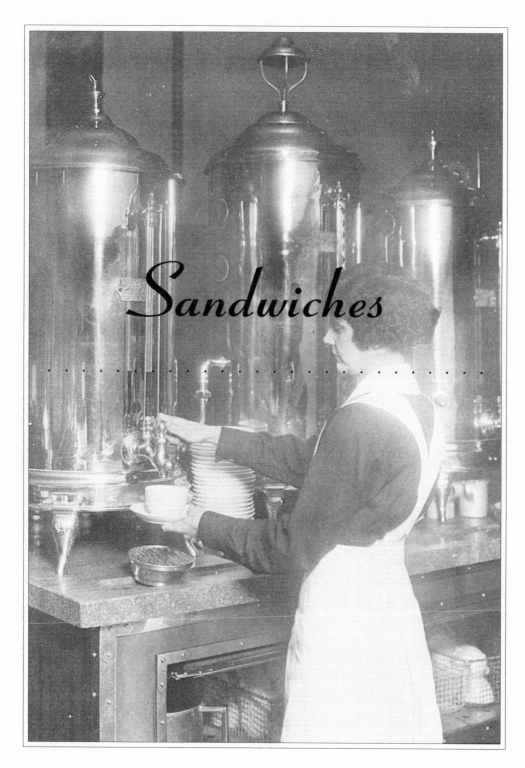

Sandwiches

Gourmet Sandwich

Ruth Tutwiler, Cafeteria Manager, Continental Building, Chicago, Illinois

. . . .

1/2 cup chopped green onions
1 cup sliced fresh mushrooms
7 tablespoons butter
8 slices (8 oz.) boiled ham
1/4 cup all-purpose flour
1/4 teaspoon salt
1 cup chicken broth
1 cup light cream
12 slices toasted white bread
6 slices processed Swiss cheese
6 thick tomato slices
1 cup shredded American cheese

Sauté onions and mushrooms in three tablespoons of butter until tender. Meanwhile cut ham into long, inch-wide strips. Melt remaining butter in a heavy saucepan, blending in salt and flour. Add chicken broth and cream gradually, stirring constantly until sauce is thick and smooth. Then add ham, onions and mushrooms. Arrange one toast slice and two diagonally cut halves into individual casseroles or a 9" x 13" baking dish. Cover each whole slice of toast with a slice of Swiss cheese. Pour sauce over all and top with tomato slice and sprinkle with American cheese. Heat under broiler until cheese melts. Serves six.

Sandwich à la Wendell

Fred Wendell, Inspector

. . . .

Bread
Chicken breast
Virginia ham
White sauce
Mushrooms
Grapefruit
Cherries
Pineapple
Pimentos

On a piece of toast lay the breast of a chicken, turkey, or guinea fowl, then a thin slice of Virginia ham, crisply broiled. Cover with a white sauce and chopped mushrooms. Serve with the following salad: Pulped grapefruit, a slice of pineapple, a sprinkle of pimentos and chopped fresh cherries. Serves one.

Monte Cristo Sandwich

William Aulder, Chef, Bright Angel Lodge, Grand Canyon, Arizona

. . . .

12 slices bread
4 slices cooked ham
4 slices processed sharp cheese
4 slices chicken breast
1 cup light cream or top milk
4 tablespoons butter
Confectioners sugar (optional)
1 egg, beaten

Make four sandwiches using three slices of bread each, with ham and cheese for one layer and chicken breast for the other layer. Combine egg and cream. Dip sandwich in egg mixture. Fry in deep fat heated to 350 degrees or in butter until brown, turning to brown both sides. Dust with confectioners sugar, if desired. Serves four. (This sandwich is also good grilled—that is, spread on outside with softened butter and browned on both sides on a griddle or electric sandwich grill. When grilled, the egg and cream dip is omitted.)

Stewart Special Sandwich

Hans Mayr, Chef, The Bowl & Bottle, Chicago, Illinois

. . . .

2 ($^1/_4$ inch) slices ham, fried
2 slices buttered toast
2 slices cheddar cheese
2 green pepper rings
Paprika

Arrange slice of ham on each slice of toast, top with cheese. Arrange two pepper rings on top of cheese, sprinkle with paprika. Broil until cheese is melted. Serve with lettuce, sweet pickle, tomato slice and French fried potatoes. Serves one.

Garnish
Lettuce
Sweet pickle
Tomato slice
French fried potatoes

145

CHAPTER NINE

The Great Terminals

· ·

The Fred Harvey company operated restaurants and other facilities in major city railway stations as well as in prairie towns. As might be expected, the first of these large operations was in Kansas City, when it became the eastern terminal of the Santa Fe. The first Santa Fe station facilities in Kansas City were not extensive, and the Fred Harvey lunchroom and dining facility were like most of the others along the line.

When the massive Kansas City Union Station opened in 1914, Ford Harvey arranged for his company to be the major concessionaire in the new facility. The scope of Fred Harvey activities encompassed not only food but also other goods and services, including restaurants, a bookstore, drug stores, gift shops, a toy store, men's and women's clothing stores, and shops or booths that handled everything from Mexican craft goods to garden supplies. One shop not expected to be found in Kansas City was the Perfume Shop, with an array and inventory equal to that of the leading stores in New York and Chicago. It became a mark of status for well-heeled travelers to use the half-hour layover period in Kansas City to purchase first-quality and expensive perfumes at the Fred Harvey shop. Local people also found that not just the perfumery but all of the Harvey shops had the best inventories of their lines in the city.

The Harvey company also pioneered in the use of mobile newsstand and specialty carts brought directly to trackside platforms to serve those passengers who did not wish to walk into the terminal itself. No potential customer was going to leave Kansas City without buying something if the Harvey folks could help it!

It's about 1930, and seven sections of the California Limited *are lined up in Los Angeles, ready to head east. That means there were enough passengers that day to fill seven full trains, most likely because of a special group trip to a convention. The photographer posed some of the passengers and crew on the cowcatchers before departure. (Heard Museum)*

As Kansas City became the company's headquarters, this complex was the crown jewel in the Harvey system. As we shall see, one Chicago station was larger, but Kansas City was generally considered the "best" of the Harvey operations, and the one to which assignments were coveted by managers and employees alike.

In 1896, on the other side of Missouri at St. Louis, the Fred Harvey presence returned to the scene of Harvey's pre–Civil War restaurant activity as part of the food-service arrangements for the St. Louis–San Francisco Railway ("Frisco"), then controlled by the Santa Fe. Harvey Houses and newsstands were placed in operation along the Frisco lines in Missouri, Oklahoma, Arkansas, Mississippi, and as far southeast as Birmingham, Alabama. These Frisco-related facilities were under Harvey operation until 1930.

In 1896, the majestic St. Louis Union Station was opened, and the Harvey restaurant along with it. The 1904 St. Louis World's Fair brought many Americans in contact with Harvey operations for the first time; letters home and newspaper clippings by the thousands attested to the quality of Fred Harvey service. During the 1920s, the Harvey company expanded operations to include the full range of retail shops.

The old dining room at Dearborn Station, Chicago. Note that in this urban setting, the tables are set for the more conventional four places. Fred Harvey china and silverware, particularly such items as the crystal decanters on the tables, are highly prized collectibles today. (Santa Fe Collections, Kansas State Historical Society)

St. Louis provides one example of employee longevity, and there were many others throughout the system. The man who developed and opened the retail operations in the 1920s, W. R. Ryan, had started with the company in 1908 as a news agent in Kansas City. Promoted to head of St. Louis commercial operations, Ryan was still on the job through the 1950s. The Harvey restaurant in St. Louis remained open until 1970, just before the coming of Amtrak.

The Harvey presence in Chicago dates back to 1899, when the company opened its first restaurant in Dearborn Station, the train shed in which Santa Fe trains began their westward journeys. Chicago, it must be remembered, was a city in which seven separate railroad passenger terminals served the many railroads entering the city; Dearborn was the Santa Fe's home.

The Harvey restaurant in Dearborn Station became known to travelers and Chicagoans alike as an outstanding eating place—not fancy, but comfortable. Here is one magazine publisher's description as late as the 1930s: "The cozy comfort of the room, the soft lights, the gleam of good walnut well cared for, the perfection of the service, the excellence of the food, and the friendly atmosphere all work together for the guests' enjoyment. This writing is not an advertisement; but it is a mark of appreciation from one who often enjoys the Harvey Hospitality and hopes to continue so doing."

Since Dearborn Station was the Santa Fe terminal, it was also the site of the Fred Harvey commissary serving the railroad dining cars. Each train departed with its diner provisioned with a carefully planned stock of quality foodstuffs, the menus and purchases having been worked out with almost military precision.

In most of the major terminal locations, the Harvey company managed not only food service operations but also retail and service shops, including barber shops, beauty salons, candy stores and soda fountains, tobacco shops, bake shops, haberdasheries, flower stands, gift shops, and other specialty stores.

The most extensive Fred Harvey concession facilities were found in another Chicago railroad terminal, Union Station, which was opened in 1925. Although the Santa Fe was not a Union Station tenant, Fred Harvey service was also installed throughout the complex. It became the largest Harvey operation, both in square footage and sales volume. Seven restaurants were opened to cater to commuters and long-distance travelers, ranging from an elegant 125-seat restaurant room to a 550-seat lunch room. Union Station also housed a Harvey bakery, which produced bread, rolls, and other goods for a series of Harvey locations besides Union Station.

Anti-smoking crusaders note: this cigar stand at Union Station no longer exists. It had the largest variety of cigars available in Kansas City. As the sign notes, Fred Harvey did a considerable mail-order business as well. (University of Arizona)

The 550-seat lunchroom at Chicago's Union Station, the largest such facility operated by Fred Harvey. (Special Collections, University of Arizona Library)

Two virtually duplicate sets of retail shops were built, one at the terminal's north end and the other at the south end. Neither cluster suffered from low patronage; in fact, when a second identical newsstand was constructed in Union Station, only two hundred feet from an existing stand, their combined sales were more than double that of the single stand.

The only major group of restaurants and service facilities that Fred Harvey operated in a railroad station east of Chicago was in Cleveland's Union Terminal, which began at the station's opening in 1930. Though the location was far from the

Santa Fe, Fred Harvey's reputation made his company the successful bidder for the restaurant and commercial complex, including a complete mezzanine of retail stores. The relationship lasted for more than forty years and came to include some other smaller operations in the Cleveland area.

The Fred Harvey presence was noteworthy in the Los Angeles Union Passenger Terminal (LAUPT), which opened in 1939 as the "Last of the Great Railway Stations." The restaurant, with twenty-seven seats at a horseshoe counter and two hundred more at booths and tables, became a well-known spot for travelers and local folks alike. Other Harvey facilities at LAUPT included a cocktail lounge, soda fountain, barber shop, news and gift stands, and a book store. Mary Colter influenced the restaurant's Spanish Provincial design and decor.

The Los Angeles Union Passenger Terminal unit was the last of the Fred Harvey terminal complexes to be opened; indeed, it was the last hurrah for the Santa Fe–Fred Harvey relationship that had begun in 1876. Some lineside facilities were already closing in the 1930s when LAUPT was constructed. Not many years later, though World War II saw a great increase in Harvey food service to railroad passengers (most of them in khaki), the decline of railway travel forced the Fred Harvey managers to look in new directions.

The Fred Harvey restaurant in LAUPT is no longer operating, but a local historical society conducts monthly tours of the restaurant area, now walled off from general view. It is still possible to stand amid the once-bustling surroundings and imagine the service and satisfaction that was generated here on a daily basis. The ghost of Fred Harvey might well be heard, uttering what were said to be his dying words: "Don't slice the ham too thin!"

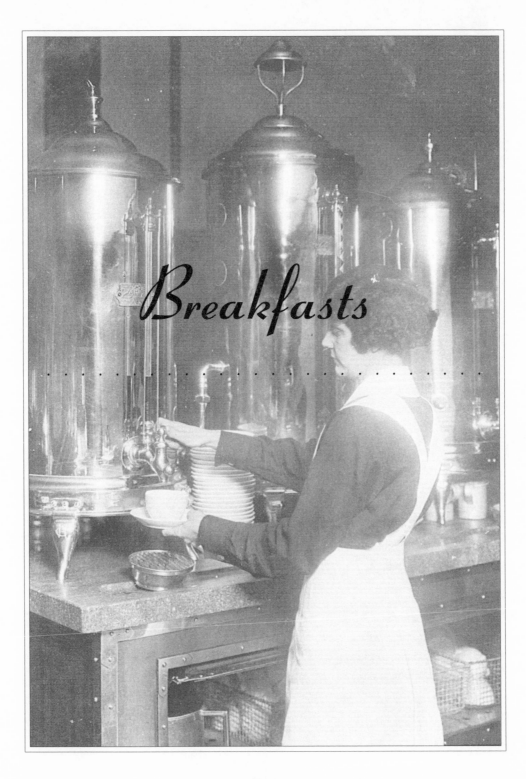

Breakfasts

Santa Fe French Toast

Hans Mayr, Research Chef, Chicago, Illinois

. . . .

1 cup light cream (half and half)
4 eggs
3 slices bread cut $1/4$ inch thick
$1/4$ teaspoon salt
Confectioners sugar
Vegetable oil

Cut firm homemade type unsliced bread into $3/4$ inch slices. Trim crusts and cut into triangles. Combine beaten eggs, cream and salt. Dip bread triangles in the mixture, allowing them to absorb as much custard as possible. Fry in about $1/2$ inch of vegetable oil pre-heated to 325 degrees. When one side is golden brown, turn and brown on the second side. Turn only once. Place on a shallow baking pan (a jelly roll pan is perfect for this) and allow to puff in a 400-degree oven for three to five minutes. Drain on paper toweling to absorb excess fat. Sprinkle with confectioners sugar and serve immediately with applesauce, currant jelly, honey, or maple syrup. Add pork sausages, bacon strips, Canadian bacon, or ham. Serves three, two triangles each.

Harvey Girl Special
Little Thin Orange Pancakes

Henry Stovall, St. Louis Union Station, Missouri

. . . .

1 cup pancake mix
1 cup orange juice (approx.)
$1/4$ cup diced orange sections
and juice ($1/2$ orange)
1 teaspoon grated orange peel
($1/2$ orange)

Combine all ingredients. Bake small pancakes on hot griddle, using one tablespoon batter for each pancake. Serve with maple syrup, honey, or jelly. Serves 12; three (2 $3/4$ inch diameter) pancakes per serving.

Huevos Rancheros, La Fonda

Konrad Allgaier, Chef, La Fonda Hotel, Santa Fe, New Mexico

. . . .

1 cup pinto beans
1 tablespoon red chili powder
¹/4 cup cold water
4 tablespoons minced onion
2 tablespoons butter
2 eggs
¹/2 to 1 teaspoon finely minced
green chili pepper
1 teaspoon butter

Wash beans, cover with cold water, and let soak over night. In the morning, heat to boiling, reduce heat and let simmer, covered, until beans are tender, three or four hours. Cool. Add red chili powder, which may be obtained from a Mexican grocery store, to the cold water and let soak one hour. Sauté onion and very finely minced green chili pepper in butter very slowly until tender but not browned. Add beans, which have been broken up coarsely with a fork, and heat through. Add ¹/4 to ¹/2 cup hot water if beans are too dry. Transfer heated beans to a well-buttered shirred egg dish or individual casserole. Make two depressions in top of beans using back of tablespoon, and drop an egg in each depression. Pour two tablespoons soaked red chili powder over the top and dot tops of eggs with butter. Bake in a moderate oven (350 degrees) for 20 to 25 minutes or until eggs are set. Serves one.

Poached Eggs à la Reine, Harlequin

Wolfgang Pschorr, Chef, Harlequin Room, Chicago, Illinois

. . . .

1 cup finely chopped mushrooms

4 tablespoons butter

1 tablespoon chopped shallots

3 tablespoons flour

1 1/4 cups top milk or cream

1/4 cup sherry

4 eggs

4 toast rounds

16 asparagus spears, cooked

Parsley

Pimento

2 pitted black olives

1 cup finely chopped chicken

(white meat)

Salt and pepper

Sauté mushrooms in butter until nearly done; add shallots and cook a few minutes longer. Blend in the flour, add top milk or cream, and cook slowly until smooth and thickened (about five minutes), stirring constantly. Add chicken and sherry. Season. Remove from heat. Poach eggs, place on round pieces of toast, and cover with the chicken and mushroom mixture. Garnish each serving with asparagus and sprigs of parsley; place strip of pimento and half of pitted black olive on each egg. Serves four.

La Fonda Pudding

Konrad Allgaier, Chef, La Fonda Hotel, Santa Fe, New Mexico

. . . .

1 cup (12) graham crackers,

finely crushed

3 egg yolks

1 cup sugar

1/2 cup chopped walnuts

1 teaspoon baking powder

1/8 teaspoon salt

1/2 teaspoon vanilla

3 egg whites, stiffly beaten

Heavy cream

Beat egg yolks until thick and lemon colored; gradually add sugar, beating constantly. Fold in graham crackers, chopped nuts, baking powder, salt, and vanilla. Fold in beaten egg whites. Bake in a buttered 8" x 8" x 2" pan in moderate oven (350 degrees) for 45 minutes. Cool pan for 10 minutes. Remove from pan. Cut into squares and serve topped with whipped cream and extra chopped walnuts if desired.

Crabapple Jam or Jelly

Dan Tachet, Chef, Castañeda, Las Vegas, New Mexico

. . . .

Crabapples
Sugar

Cut the crabapples in quarters, removing the affected parts. Put them in a pot with enough water to cover them; let boil until well done; then put them in a bag and press out the juice as much as possible. To six quarts of liquid add five of sugar, mix well and let cook until it will coat a wooden spoon or will jell quickly when dropped on a cold plate. For jam, pass the thick part of the apples (all but the skin and seeds) through a sieve. To six quarts of pulp add 3 quarts of sugar; mix well and cook for about three hours, stirring frequently; pour into jars while hot.

Concord Grape Jelly

Dan Tachet, Chef, Castañeda, Las Vegas, New Mexico

. . . .

Green grapes
Sugar

Green or half green grapes must be used. Put them on a fire with water enough to cover the bottom of the pan. Let them cook 10 or 15 minutes and strain every drop through a cloth. Add to the juice an equal proportion of granulated sugar, cook like crabapple jelly, and put in glasses or jars. Let stand a few days in an airy place; cover the jars with melted paraffin and set away in cool place.

Quince Jam or Jelly

Dan Tachet, Chef, Castañeda, Las Vegas, New Mexico

. . . .

Quinces
Sugar

For jam or jelly, quince may be treated exactly as crabapples, except that they require longer cooking and consequently more water.

Fred Harvey Coffee

· ·

The secrets of good coffee are that it be 1) made strong enough, 2) served hot enough, 3) brewed correctly, 4) always freshly made, and 5) made from good coffee.

Drip Coffee

Use one rounded tablespoon of regular grind to each six-ounce cup of fresh boiling water. Scald your coffee pot with boiling water. Put coffee in coffee basket, replace in pot and cover with water container. Slowly pour boiling water into it. Keep warm while coffee drips through, then remove upper sections, stir, cover pot, and serve.

Percolator Coffee

Use one heaping tablespoon of regular grind to each six-ounce cup of water. Measure water into percolator. Wet coffee basket with water, add coffee and insert basket in pot. Bring to boil, reduce heat, and allow to percolate gently from seven to ten minutes after percolating starts. When desired strength is reached, remove basket, cover, and serve.

Glass Coffee Maker

Measure water into lower bowl, allowing six ounces of water for each cup, and bring to a fast boil. Meantime, measure coffee into upper bowl, allowing 1 rounded tablespoon of fine-grind coffee per cup. When water boils, place upper bowl on lower and return to heat. When water has risen, stir carefully; reduce heat for four minutes. Remove from heat, separate bowls, cover, and serve.

Automatic Coffee Maker

Measure water into the lower bowl, allowing six ounces of water for each cup. Allow one rounded tablespoon of fine-grind coffee per cup, which should be placed in upper part of automatic coffee maker. The rest of the procedure is, of course, automatic.

CHAPTER TEN

Change of Focus

· ·

Despite the quality of their food and service, the Santa Fe railside Harvey Houses large and small fell victim to technology and economics. True, the depression figured into the railroad's decisions, but the major reason for declining Harvey House patronage was that trains were becoming longer, heavier, and faster, and they needed to make far fewer stops. The Harvey-operated on-board diners thus replaced meal stops.

Just as Fred Harvey had revolutionized food service on the railroads in the 1800s, so in 1929, his descendants and his company participated in another revolutionary transportation service—across the continent by air and rail. At that time, a cross-country rail trip took at least four days. The Santa Fe and Pennsylvania railroads and a small company called Transcontinental Air Transport (TAT) joined forces to cut that transcontinental travel time to forty-eight hours. Such speed across country was then unheard of; after all, it was only two years earlier that Charles Lindbergh had soloed across the Atlantic. But that same Charles Lindbergh was TAT's chief pilot, planning the routes and hiring the flight personnel.

The coast-to-coast service involved flying aboard one of TAT's fifteen-passenger Ford Trimotors by day and traveling by train overnight. Airports didn't have lights or navigation aids back then, and night flying, particularly in mountainous areas, was considered unsafe. A passenger in New York who sought to journey to California boarded a train at Pennsylvania Station at 6:00 P.M., enjoying the comforts of diner, lounge, and Pullman until the train reached Columbus, Ohio, early the next morning. At Port Columbus, one or more Trimotors were waiting to take off within minutes of the train's arrival. Lunch aloft the plane was the first meal by Fred Harvey

The steward is attentively providing Fred Harvey meal service on board a Transcontinental Air Transport Trimotor. The Harvey Standard for quality was upheld, even in midair. (Smithsonian Institution)

that the passengers experienced, and it was indeed a full meal.

By early evening, the plane reached Waynoka, Oklahoma, where the passengers were transported to the Harvey House for dinner. After dinner, the westward journey continued on a Santa Fe Railroad overnight train that arrived at Clovis, New Mexico, the next morning, just in time for breakfast at the Harvey House. After breakfast, passengers boarded another Trimotor, enjoyed another Fred Harvey lunch in midair, and arrived in Los Angeles just before 6:00 P.M.

The service was truly first class; the $350 cost was about double the regular first-class train fare. As operators of the supersonic *Concorde* were to prove later on, the improvement in travel time was deemed to be worth the cost to a number of people. But not enough people, since the service was stopped after about fifteen months because of unprofitability. Larger planes would have helped, but by the time larger planes became available, those newer aircraft also had longer range capabilities, making the rail connections less essential.

The venture with Transcontinental Air Transport (later known as Trans World Airlines) propelled the Harvey company into airline feeding, centered at the

Two Constellations and a DC-3 await their next flights at Albuquerque Airport, from which Fred Harvey meals were supplied for on-board service. The former Transcontinental Air Transport, later named Trans World Airlines, maintained the Fred Harvey connection established in 1929. (Albuquerque Museum Photoarchives)

Albuquerque airport. In-flight and airport meals made up that Harvey division. For a number of years, Harvey meals were served aboard midwestern and Rocky Mountain airline trips. As one of the authors can attest personally, the Harvey food was indeed good enough to cause passengers to select the Harvey-supplied airline over others wherever possible. Regrettably, that airline no longer exists.

Fred Harvey service even reached bus transport, for a while. In California, Fred Harvey restaurants were built into the Santa Fe's two bus terminals, in Los Angeles and in San Francisco. These restaurants became more successful after Harvey carpenters walled them off from direct contact with the bus terminals, as an upscale clientele, more in keeping with Fred Harvey service and pricing, was attracted. One Harvey executive explained the reason for the change this way: "Bus passengers eat; they don't dine." Clearly, this was a different market, and a different economy.

But the best days of the Fred Harvey system were numbered. The first casualties were the lineside Harvey Houses, made obsolete by faster trains with on-board dining cars. This wave of cutbacks occurred during the 1930s, with closings of Harvey hotels and restaurants in smaller towns. Many of the buildings were left standing, which became a boon to the Santa Fe and the war effort in World War II. Reopening some of the restaurants, the Santa Fe called Harvey Girls back from retirement to serve soldiers and sailors on troop trains.

After the war, a second wave of cutbacks and closings was much more severe. Virtually nothing survived of the original Harvey system except the major terminal restaurants and resort hotels. Except for the Alvarado, supported by a growing urban area around the station, the major hotel facilities that survived the cutbacks of the 1930s and 1940s were the ones located away from the Santa Fe main line, namely the Grand Canyon complex (including El Tovar) and La Fonda at Santa Fe.

The most significant casualty of World War II was the Harvey standard of service itself. Just before the war, the company estimated that its service capacity was 30,000 people a day. During the war that number climbed to 60,000 servings per day. The Harvey standard was impossible to maintain in that overloaded condition. Almost all of the old Harvey employees point to the overwhelming wartime crowds and the government-controlled food and price regulations as the causes of deterioration of the first-class Fred Harvey service.

One offshoot of the restaurant operations in Chicago's railway terminals was a group of twelve restaurants that Fred Harvey operated in the Chicago area, as well as on-premises contract food service within industrial and commercial buildings. Including the Kungsholm, Continental Club, and the Old Spinning Wheel, the restaurants were a natural extension in what had become the Harvey headquarters city. Highway travelers experienced Fred Harvey service, too, at rest-area and restaurant locations along the Illinois Tollway. Even as late as the early 1960s, the combined Fred Harvey facilities in the Chicago area alone could seat 5,000 people simultaneously.

An array of other restaurant and food service operations operated under the Fred Harvey banner from Ohio to California, including facilities at California's Painted Desert. But the era of the unified service provided by the Harvey Houses, served by their own fleet of refrigerator express railcars and bound by a common purpose, was virtually gone by the 1950s, along with the classic railroad passenger train itself.

The Amtrak service, which began in 1971, including food service characterized by vending machines and "snack bars," is clearly of a different era. However, the memories of dining elegance in the West persist. Perhaps Elbert Hubbard said it best in his eulogy of Fred Harvey, voicing a sentiment that Harvey's descendants maintained for many years thereafter:

> Fred Harvey is dead, but his spirit still lives. The standard of excellence he set can never go back. He has been a civilizer and a benefactor. He has added to the physical, mental and spiritual welfare of millions. I take my hat off to Fred Harvey, who served the patrons of the Santa Fe so faithfully and well that, dying, he yet lives, his name a symbol of all that is honest, excellent, hygienic, beautiful and useful.

Fred Harvey and his descendants created what became the most famous and successful restaurant and hotel chain in America, in cooperation with a series of Santa Fe railroad managers who allowed it to happen, in the interest of their customers.

Consumer surveys still rank the Santa Fe at the top of the U.S. railroads in terms of positive recognition, and the Santa Fe Railway is still known as a company with an above-average record of excellence. The lunch rooms, Harvey Houses, Santa Fe Railroad Hotels, and the great passenger trains with their elegant dining cars, are gone; but the spirit that gave us the Fred Harvey tradition survives. Occasional reunions of former Harvey Girls and other employees demonstrate the strong psychological bond that unites them even as the inexorable passage of time causes their numbers to dwindle.

You hold in your hand what is perhaps the most tangible part of the Fred Harvey legacy, a collection of recipes that represent some of the most outstanding dining that America had to offer between 1876 and the 1950s, "recipes that civilized the American West."

We hope that this book will help you to recapture the memories of those elegant meals.

Sauces

Frankfurter Sauce

Nelle Smith, Test Kitchen Supervisor

- -

¹/₂ cup catsup
¹/₄ cup chili sauce
1 tablespoon horseradish
¹/₄ cup prepared mustard
¹/₄ cup sweet pickle relish

Mix all ingredients together; spoon on franks. This sauce is also good on hamburgers or cheeseburgers.

Sauce for Ham

Nelle Smith, Test Kitchen Supervisor

- -

1 cup orange juice
¹/₂ cup water
¹/₂ cup brown sugar
1 tablespoon honey
2 teaspoons lemon juice

Place all ingredients in pan and bring to a rolling boil. Remove from fire and use to baste the ham. Also good on sweet potatoes.

Red Chili Sauce

Eli Gomez, Chef , Bright Angel Lodge, Grand Canyon, Arizona

- -

8 oz. frozen red chili
1 clove garlic, chopped
1 onion, chopped

Combine eight ounces (thawed) red chili with one chopped onion and one clove chopped garlic. Cook 10 minutes. Strain. Six servings.

Basic Medium White Sauce

2 tablespoons fat
(butter, margarine, or drippings)
2 tablespoons flour
1 cup milk
$^1/_4$ teaspoon salt
Pinch pepper

Melt two tablespoons of fat in a small saucepan over low heat. Blend in two tablespoons of flour to form a smooth paste. Slowly stir in one cup of milk and heat, stirring constantly, until the mixture has thickened and is smooth. Add $^1/_4$ teaspoon of salt and a pinch of pepper, and allow it to mellow about five minutes, stirring occasionally over low heat. Yield: one cup.

Basic Tomato Sauce

G. Hoagland Foster

3 $^1/_2$ cups crushed tomatoes
3 tablespoons olive oil
1 cup finely chopped onions
Salt
6 tablespoons tomato paste
Pepper
1 $^1/_2$ teaspoons crushed oregano
1 cup beef stock
$^1/_4$ teaspoons hot red pepper flakes
1 $^1/_2$ tablespoons minced garlic
6 tablespoons finely chopped basil
$^1/_4$ cup finely chopped parsley
1 tablespoon powered orange rind

Heat the olive oil in a saucepan; add the onion and garlic and cook briefly while stirring. Do not brown. Add the crushed tomatoes, tomato paste, oregano, red pepper flakes, salt, pepper, basil, parsley, and orange rind. Stir and bring to the boil. Add stock and let simmer for 30 minutes.

Espagñole Sauce

4 slices of bacon, minced
1 stalk celery, minced
1 medium yellow onion, minced
1 medium carrot, minced
6 tablespoons butter
6 tablespoons flour
5 cups beef broth
Pinch of thyme
$^1/_2$ bay leaf
$^1/_4$ cup tomato purée

Stir-fry bacon over moderate heat three to four minutes; drain on paper towels. Sauté onion, carrot, and celery in drippings eight to ten minutes until golden and drain. Melt butter in a saucepan over moderate heat, blend in flour, then cook and stir one to two minutes until lightly brown. Slowly mix in the beef broth and cook, stirring constantly, until slightly thickened. Add bacon, tomato purée, the cooked vegetables, and herbs. Reduce heat and boil uncovered very slowly for half an hour, skimming light scum from the sides of the pan as it collects. Strain sauce through a fine sieve into a clean saucepan, pressing vegetables. Yields about 2 $^2/_3$ cups.

Demi-Glace Rich Brown Sauce

1 cup beef broth
$^1/_4$ cup dry Madeira or sherry
Espagnole Sauce

Mix Espagnole Sauce and beef broth and boil slowly, uncovered, until reduced to three cups. (Sauce should coat metal spoon.) Mix in wine and serve, or use as a base for other sauces. Yields 3 $^1/_4$ cups.

Perigueux Sauce

2 tablespoons minced truffles
1 cup Rich Brown Sauce
(Demi-Glace)

Mix two tablespoons of minced truffles into one cup Rich Brown Sauce. Yield one cup. Serve with Chicken Breast Tenerife au Grand Marnier.

Bordelaise Sauce

. . . .

1 recipe Rich Brown Sauce

2 cups dry red wine

1/4 teaspoon dried thyme

1/2 cup bone marrow

2 tablespoons minced shallots or
white part scallions

1 small bay leaf

1 tablespoon minced parsley

Prepare Rich Brown Sauce and keep warm. Boil two cups dry red wine, uncovered, with two tablespoons minced shallots or scallion whites, thyme, and bay leaf until reduced to one 1/3 cup. Strain wine into sauce and simmer, uncovered, until reduced to one quart. Mix in 1/2 cup minced marrow from bones and one tablespoon minced parsley. Use salt as needed to taste. Yield: one quart. Serve with Beef Steak Frascati.

Bearnaise Sauce

. . . .

1/4 cup dry white wine

1/4 cup white wine vinegar

1 tablespoon minced tarragon★

1 tablespoon minced chervil★

1 tablespoon minced shallots or
scallions (white part only)

1/8 teaspoon salt

Pinch of white pepper

1/2 teaspoon tarragon

1/2 teaspoon chervil

Boil the wine, vinegar, one tablespoon of fresh tarragon and chervil, shallots, salt, and pepper together until the liquid reduces to two tablespoons. Strain liquid and allow to cool to room temperature. Prepare Hollandaise as directed, substituting the reduced liquid for the lemon juice. Before you serve, mix in 1/2 teaspoon of fresh tarragon and 1/2 teaspoon of fresh chervil. Yields about 1 1/3 cups.

★ If dried is used, cut amount by half

Sauce Robert

. . . .

1 large yellow onion, minced
2 tablespoons butter
1 cup dry white wine
$^1/_4$ teaspoon sugar
1 $^1/_2$ teaspoons powered mustard
1 teaspoon cold water
Rich Brown Sauce

Sauté one minced onion in two tablespoons butter for five to eight minutes over moderate heat until the onion is pale golden. Add one cup of dry white wine and boil, uncovered, until reduced to $^1/_2$ cup. Stir into Rich Brown Sauce along with $^1/_4$ teaspoon of sugar and 1 $^1/_2$ teaspoons powdered mustard blended with one teaspoon cold water. Simmer, uncovered, for 20 minutes. Yields one quart.

Marco Polo Sauce

Lewis Eklich, Chef, Cleveland Union Terminal Restaurants

. . . .

1 cup minced onions
1 cup minced celery
$^1/_2$ lemon, finely minced
2 minced scallions
6 strips diced bacon
2 cups beef stock
1 tablespoon roux
1 small minced leek
$^2/_3$ cup A-1 sauce
1 teaspoon horseradish
1 $^1/_2$ cup chili sauce
1 teaspoon curry powder
$^2/_3$ cup Escoffier Sauce Robert
1 teaspoon soy sauce

Sauté bacon, onion, scallions, celery, and leek in skillet. Then add soy sauce, chili, A-1, and Escoffier sauce and simmer for one hour. Add lemon and curry powder, blend, add horseradish and beef stock, and finally thicken with roux. Serve with Tournedos of Beef, Marco Polo.

Cumberland Sauce

2 tablespoons orange rind
1 tablespoon lemon rind
1 shallot minced or scallion,
white part
$^1/_2$ cup of water
1 cup red currant jelly
1 cup Tawny Port wine
$^1/_4$ cup orange juice
2 tablespoons lemon juice
$^1/_2$ teaspoon powdered mustard
mixed with 1 tablespoon water
$^1/_2$ teaspoon salt
$^1/_8$ teaspoon ginger
Pinch cayenne pepper

Boil the orange and lemon rinds, shallots or scallions, and salt in $^1/_2$ cup of water for three or four minutes. Drain off the water. Add currant jelly, wine, mustard, orange and lemon juices, salt, ginger, and cayenne pepper. Simmer for 10 minutes covered and allow to rest for five minutes. Yields two cups.

Madeira Sauce

1 cup Rich Brown Sauce
$^1/_4$ cup Madeira wine

Mix the Rich Brown Sauce and the Madeira wine, allow to simmer for three or four minutes, and serve. Yields about one cup.

Sauce Supreme

Chester Gerlich, Chef, Harvey House, Riverside Plaza, Chicago, Illinois

. . . .

1/4 cup shortening

1/2 cup all-purpose flour

2 1/2 pints chicken stock

1/2 teaspoon lemon juice

1/2 tablespoon butter (solid form)

Salt to taste

Egg (yellow) coloring

Blend flour into shortening over low heat. Cook slowly until flour and shortening mixture is smooth. Stir in warm chicken stock, stirring constantly until well blended and boiling. Continue to boil over low heat for 45 minutes to one hour. Add lemon juice and salt. With wire whip, stir in egg (yellow) coloring to give sauce a rich, creamy appearance. Stir in butter and remove from fire. Strain through fine sieve. Yields one quart. Serve with Chicken Poulette.

Note: Lemon juice should be used only when using real chicken stock.

Fricassee Sauce

. . . .

3 tablespoons butter

1/4 cup unsifted flour

2 cups chicken broth

1 egg yolk

1/2 cup cream

1 teaspoon lemon juice

1/4 teaspoon sugar

3/4 teaspoon salt

Mix egg yolk and cream and hold. Melt the butter in a medium sauce pan over moderate heat, blend in flour, and slowly stir in the broth, stirring until thickened. Mix a little of the flour mixture into the yolk mixture, and add to the sauce and stir. Blend in the lemon juice, sugar, and salt. Adjust for taste. Yield: about three cups.

Bechamel Sauce

4 tablespoon butter (no substitutes)

1/4 cup unsifted flour

2 cups milk*

1/2 teaspoon salt (approx.)

1/8 teaspoon white pepper

2 tablespoons minced yellow onion

2 oz. ground veal★★

1/4 bay leaf

Pinch of nutmeg

1 small sprig of fresh thyme or
a pinch of dried

★ or 1 cup milk and 1 cup either
chicken, fish, or vegetable broth

★★ 2 oz. ground veal if sauce is
used for meat or poultry

Melt three tablespoons of butter in a double boiler top over direct moderate heat; slowly blend in flour, add milk, and stir until thickened. Add salt and pepper and set over simmering water. Fry onion in one tablespoon of butter three to five minutes, over moderate heat, until limp. (Add veal if sauce is for meat or poultry and cook until no longer pink; add to sauce along with the remaining ingredients). Cover and cook for an hour over simmering water. Beat with a whisk now and then and use a spatula to scrape sides and bottom. Strain sauce, adjust for salt. Note: when removing the lid, take care not to let condensed water drop into the sauce. Yield: 1 $^2/3$ cups.

Chili Sauce

6 tomatoes

4 green peppers, minced

1 onion, minced

1 teaspoon sugar

1 teaspoon salt

1/2 cup vinegar

Cut up the tomatoes, add all the ingredients, boil for an hour, and then strain. Yields about one cup.

Chili Sauce

Dan Tachet, Chef, Castañeda, Las Vegas, New Mexico

. . . .

10 oz. dry red chili
Water
1 sliced onion
1 clove garlic, crushed
2 oz. sugar
Salt
1 quart water or 1 quart tomatoes,
finely chopped
1 tablespoon cornstarch

Take 10 ounces of dry red chili, free from seeds and veins. Set in the oven for five minutes to make them crisp, being careful not to burn them. Soak in plenty of water for two hours, drain and put them on the stove, with one sliced onion, one crushed clove of garlic, two ounces of sugar, a little salt and one quart of water. Let boil 15 minutes. Dissolve about a tablespoonful of cornstarch in a little water, add it to the boiling chili and strain until every particle of pulp is forced out of the chili. Mix well and season to taste. The foregoing is a Mexican sauce, but the average American prefers a somewhat milder sauce, which can be produced by one quart or more of tomatoes instead of water.

Hollandaise Sauce

. . . .

1/2 cup sweet butter (one stick)
3 large egg yolks
Pinch of salt
Pinch of cayenne pepper
2 to 2 1/2 tablespoons fresh
lemon juice
1 to 2 tablespoons boiling water

Use a double boiler set over simmering (never boiling) water. Cut the butter into three equal parts. Place one piece of butter into the top of the double boiler and add egg yolks, beating with a whisk or wooden spoon until the butter is completely melted. Add the next two pieces of butter one at a time, beating each until melted. Add the lemon juice, salt, and cayenne pepper, and continue to beat about 10 to 12 minutes, until the sauce is the consistency of heavy cream. Add a tablespoon or two of boiling water. Taste to adjust seasonings. (You may want to add more cayenne pepper or lemon juice.) Yields about one cup. Serve with Pompano en Papillon.

Sauce Chantilly

Carl Burger, Chef, Palmolive Building Restaurants, Chicago, Illinois

Butter
Flour
White wine
1 cup Hollandaise Sauce
1 cup whipped cream

Bring liquid in saucepan to a boil and thicken with a little beurre manié (equal parts butter and flour kneaded together). Then boil a few minutes and strain sauce. Add one cup Hollandaise Sauce and $^1/_2$ cup whipped cream. Serve with Fruit de Mer, Madame Pompadour.

Punch Sauce

$^1/_4$ lb. butter
1 $^1/_3$ cups sifted confectioners sugar
Dash of salt
1 egg, separated
2 tablespoons cognac
$^1/_2$ cup heavy cream, whipped
Pinch of grated nutmeg

Soften the butter and gradually blend in the sugar. Add the salt and egg yolk and beat well. Cook over hot, not boiling, water, stirring constantly, until the mixture is light and fluffy, about six to seven minutes. Remove from the heat and stir in the cognac. Chill. Fold in the egg white; beaten until it stands in soft peaks. Fold in the whipped cream just before serving. Sprinkle with nutmeg. Yields about two cups.

Mustard Sauce

$^1/_4$ cup prepared mustard
1 to 2 teaspoons cider vinegar
1 cup Medium White Sauce

Into one cup of Medium White Sauce blend $^1/_4$ cup prepared mustard and one to two teaspoons cider vinegar; let blend, stirring occasionally over lowest heat for five minutes before serving. Yield: 1 $^1/_4$ cups.

Beurre Manié

. . . .

3 tablespoons butter
2 tablespoons flour

Blend softened butter and flour until smooth. Pinch off small pieces and add one at a time, stirring constantly, to hot liquids, gravies, and sauces to thicken. Yields about three tablespoons.

Veloute Sauce

. . . .

6 tablespoons butter (no substitute)
6 tablespoons flour
2 cups chicken broth★
¹/₄ teaspoon salt (approx.)
Pinch of pepper
2 to 3 tablespoons coarsely chopped mushrooms (optional)

★ If the veloute is to be used for poultry, egg, or vegetable dishes, make with chicken broth; if to be used with meat, use veal stock; if used with seafood, fish stock.

Melt butter in a heavy saucepan over moderate heat. Blend in flour, gradually stir in broth, and heat, stirring constantly, until thick and smooth. Add seasonings and mushrooms, reduce heat, and simmer uncovered for a half hour, stirring often and skimming light scum from sides of the pan as it collects. Turn heat to lowest point, cover, and simmer for a half hour, stirring now and then. Strain sauce through a fine sieve. Yields 1 ¹/₃ cups. Note: When uncovering sauce, don't let moisture on lid drop into sauce.

White Chaud-Froid Sauce

. . . .

1 ¹/₃ cup Veloute Sauce
1 cup chicken broth
¹/₃ cup heavy cream
1 pkg. gelatin (approx.)

Reduce the veloute in a heavy non–aluminum saucepan. During the reduction, whisk in the chicken broth and two tablespoons of the heavy cream. Reduce down to about 1 ²/₃ cups. Stir constantly during reduction. Strain and then whisk in the remaining heavy cream. Allow the sauce to cool to room temperature. Then paint a thin layer on a chilled plate. Refrigerate the plate briefly (five to ten minutes) to see if the sauce gels easily. If a solid gel has not set, reheat the sauce and stir in the package of gelatin. Heat until the gelatin has been completely dissolved. Cool. Chill sauce until just barely pourable. It is now ready to use. Yields about 1 ¹/₃ cups.

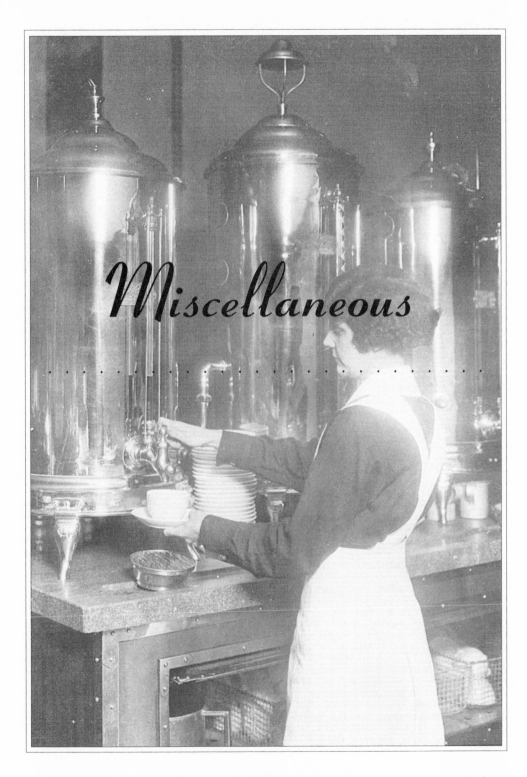

Miscellaneous

Ham Rarebit

Nelle Smith, Test Kitchen Supervisor

. . . .

¹/₃ cup butter
1 cup ham, diced
2 tablespoons flour
1 teaspoon dry mustard
1 teaspoon Worcestershire sauce
1 cup cream
1 ¹/₂ cup sharp cheese, grated
Few grains cayenne pepper
2 tablespoons white wine or stale beer
Toast

Melt butter, stir in flour, blend well. Add mustard; slowly stir in cream. Stir in grated cheese, cook slowly until cheese is melted. Add Worcestershire, pepper, and the wine or beer. Blend well. Stir in diced ham. This may be prepared ahead of time and held over hot water, or all prepared before your guests in your chafing dish. A dash of paprika over the top gives color. Serve on toast.

Swiss Fondue

Klaus Rubeck, Chef, Old Spinning Wheel, Hinsdale, Illinois

. . . .

2 cups white wine
3 teaspoons cornstarch
3 tablespoons Kirsch
1 clove fresh garlic
Nutmeg to taste
French bread
1 lb. Swiss cheese,
shredded or finely cut

Rub casserole with garlic. Pour in wine and heat to simmering. Then add cheese, stirring constantly with a wooden spoon until cheese begins to melt. Add cornstarch dissolved in Kirsch and nutmeg. Serve bubbling hot. Spear small chunks of French bread with a fork through crust, dunk, and swirl in fondue. Keep at simmering temperature! Instead of all Swiss cheese you may substitute a half pound of Swiss cheese and a half pound of Gruyere. (May also be used as an appetizer.) Serves four.

Fred Harvey Operation Locations

· ·

Compiled from many official and unofficial sources, this is the most comprehensive list of Fred Harvey operating locations known to exist. Surviving Fred Harvey and Santa Fe Railroad company records formed the foundation, but they were incomplete. Supplemental information has been gathered from newspaper clippings, official guides, timetables, advertising flyers, and local historical publications.

There is little information surviving on the nature, extent, or duration of Fred Harvey facilities along the Frisco route. Since Fred Harvey operated food services on that line during the period when the Frisco was under Santa Fe control, we can estimate generally that Harvey operations on the Frisco began in 1896 and ended in 1930. This period, of course, does not necessarily apply to each individual location.

The list of "Later" Harvey operations is also incomplete, partly due to the ephemeral nature of the restaurant business, in which operating units begin with much fanfare and go out with little or none.

Obviously, any additions or corrections to this information would be much appreciated.

Railroad Abbreviations

ATSF	Atchison, Topeka and Santa Fe
GCSF	Gulf Coast and Santa Fe
KP	Kansas Pacific
SLSF	St. Louis–San Francisco (Frisco)
TRRA	Terminal Railroad Association of St. Louis

Fred Harvey Railroad-related Operations

CITY	RAILROAD	HOTEL/RESTAURANT	OPEN	CLOSE
Alabama				
Birmingham	SLSF		1896	1930
Arkansas				
Fayetteville	SLSF			
Fort Smith	SLSF			
Jonesboro	SLSF			
Rogers	SLSF			
Arizona				
Ash Fork	ATSF	Escalante Hotel	1895	1948
Del Rio	ATSF	Farm complex		
Grand Canyon	ATSF	El Tovar, Bright Angel, Phantom Ranch, etc.	1903	
Holbrook	ATSF	(temporary, five boxcars)		c. 1888
Kingman	ATSF			
Painted Desert Inn	ATSF			
Peach Springs	ATSF	Dairy Farm		
Phoenix	ATSF			
Seligman	ATSF	The Havasu Hotel	1913	
Skull Valley	ATSF			
Williams	ATSF	Fray Marcos 1905	1887	1948
Winslow	ATSF	La Posada Hotel 1928	1887	1957
California				
Baghdad	ATSF			
Bakersfield	ATSF			
Barstow	ATSF	Casa del Desierto 1910	1887	1959
Daggett	ATSF			
Fresno	ATSF			
Los Angeles (Old)	ATSF		1900	1939
Los Angeles UPT	ATSF	restaurants, shops	1939	1980
Merced	ATSF			
Mojave	ATSF			
Needles	ATSF	El Garces Hotel 1901	1887	1948

CITY	RAILROAD	HOTEL/RESTAURANT	OPEN	CLOSE
Oceanside	ATSF			
San Bernardino	ATSF			1887
San Diego	ATSF			1910
San Francisco	ATSF	Ferry Building newsstand		
San Francisco ferry	ATSF	*Ocean Wave*		
San Francisco ferry	ATSF	*San Pablo*		
San Francisco Bus	ATSF	restaurant		
Stockton	ATSF			
Colorado				
Colorado Springs	ATSF	hotel		
Hugo	KP			
La Junta	ATSF	El Otero Hotel 1901	1880	1948
Palmer Lake	ATSF			
Pueblo	ATSF			c. 1888
Trinidad	ATSF	Cardinas Hotel 1895	1888	1933
Iowa				
Fort Madison	ATSF			
Illinois				
Chicago Dearborn Station	ATSF	restaurants, shops	1899	
Chicago Union Station		restaurants, shops	1925	
Chillicothe	ATSF			
East St. Louis	SLSF	Relay Station		
Galesburg	ATSF			
Streator	ATSF			
Kansas				
Arkansas City	ATSF		1883	1933
Augusta	ATSF			1887
Chanute	ATSF			1931
Concordia	ATSF			c. 1888

CITY	RAILROAD	HOTEL/RESTAURANT	OPEN	CLOSE
Coolidge	ATSF			1880
Dodge City	ATSF	El Vaquero 1900	1888	1948
Elk Falls	ATSF			c. 1888
Emporia	ATSF	hotel	1888	
Florence	ATSF	Santa Fe Hotel	1878	1901
Fort Scott	SLSF			1896
Halstead	ATSF			c. 1888
Hutchinson	ATSF	Bisonte Hotel 1906	1883	1946
Kinsley	ATSF			
Lakin	ATSF	(restaurant moved to Coolidge)	1879	1880
Lawrence	ATSF			
Lawrence	KP			
Lyons	ATSF			c. 1888
Madison	ATSF			c. 1888
Manchester	ATSF			c. 1888
McPherson	ATSF			c. 1888
Ness City	ATSF			
Newton	ATSF	Arcade Hotel	1871	1930
Ottawa	ATSF			c. 1888
Pittsburg	ATSF			
Rush Center	ATSF			c. 1887
Sawyer	ATSF			c. 1888
Spivey	ATSF			c. 1888
Syracuse	ATSF	Sequoyah Hotel 1908		1936
Topeka	ATSF		1876	1940
Wallace	KP	Wallace Hotel		
Wellington	ATSF	Santa Fe Hotel	1883	
Wichita	ATSF			1935
Winfield	ATSF			c. 1888
Missouri				
Cape Girardeau	SLSF			
Joplin	SLSF			
Kansas City	ATSF & SLSF	restaurants, shops		
Lawson	ATSF			

CITY	RAILROAD	HOTEL/RESTAURANT	OPEN	CLOSE
Marceline	ATSF			
Monett	SLSF	hotel		
Newburg	SLSF			
Pierce City	SLSF			c. 1886
Springfield	SLSF	restaurant, commissary		
St. Louis Union Station	TRRA	restaurants, shops	1896	1970
Tower Grove	SLSF		1886	1930
Mississippi				
Amory	SLSF			
New Mexico				
Albuquerque	ATSF	Alvarado Hotel 1899	1883	1969
Belen	ATSF			
Clovis	ATSF	Gran Quivera 1900	1883	1948
Deming	ATSF			
Deming Union Station	ATSF & SP	hotel	1883	1929
Gallup	ATSF	El Navajo Hotel 1923	1895	1957
Lamy	ATSF	El Ortiz 1910	1883	1938
Las Cruces	ATSF			
Las Vegas (resort)	ATSF	Montezuma	1882	1901
Las Vegas (trackside)	ATSF	Castañeda 1898	1882	1948
Raton	ATSF			
Rincon	ATSF	Santa Fe Hotel	1883	1933
San Marcial	ATSF	Santa Fe Hotel (flooded out)	1883	1930
Santa Fe	ATSF	La Fonda Hotel 1926	1883	1968
Vaughn	ATSF	Las Chavez 1910	1883	1936
Wallace	ATSF			1883
Ohio				
Cleveland Union Terminal		restaurants, shops	1930	

CITY	RAILROAD	HOTEL/RESTAURANT	OPEN	CLOSE
Oklahoma				
Afton	SLSF			
Antlers	SLSF	railroad hotel		
Ardmore	ATSF & SLSF			
Bartlesville	ATSF			
Claremore	SLSF			
Enid	ATSF			
Francis	SLSF			
Guthrie	ATSF			
Henryetta	SLSF			
Hugo	SLSF			
Madill	SLSF			
Miami	SLSF			
Muskogee	SLSF			
Oklahoma City	ATSF & SLSF			
Okmulgee	SLSF			
Purcell	ATSF			
Sapulpa	SLSF	railroad hotel		
Snyder	ATSF			
Tallahina			1893	
Tulsa	ATSF & SLSF			
Vinita	SLSF			
Waynoka	ATSF			
Woodward	ATSF			c. 1888
Tennessee				
Memphis	SLSF			
Texas				
Amarillo	ATSF	railroad hotel		
Beaumont	ATSF			
Bovina	ATSF			1904
Brownwood	ATSF			1938
Canadian	ATSF	railroad hotel		
Cleburne	GCSF			1931

CITY	RAILROAD	HOTEL/RESTAURANT	OPEN	CLOSE
Dallas (Old Union)	ATSF & SLSF			1923
El Paso	ATSF		1906	1948
Fort Worth	ATSF			1933
Gainesville	ATSF			1931
Galveston (I)	GCSF			1897
Galveston (II)	GCSF			1938
Goldthwaite	ATSF			
Houston	GCSF			1911
Ladonia	ATSF			c. 1887
Lometa	ATSF			1893
Milano	ATSF			1889
Navasota	ATSF			c. 1887
Panhandle	ATSF			1899
Paris	ATSF & SLSF		1896	1930
Rosenberg	GCSF			
Silsbee	ATSF	railroad hotel		1923
Slaton	ATSF			
Somerville	GCSF	Santa Fe Hotel		
Sweetwater	ATSF	cottages		1933
Temple	GCSF	hotel, farm	1933	
Valley Mills	ATSF			c. 1888

Later Harvey Operations

CITY	HOTEL/RESTAURANT	OPEN	CLOSE
Arizona			
Cameron	Cameron Trading Post		
Petrified National Forest	Painted Desert Oasis		
Phoenix	Green Gables Restaurant		
Winslow	TAT/TWA in-flight		

CITY	HOTEL/RESTAURANT	OPEN	CLOSE
California			
Barstow	Harvey House Restaurant	1966	
Burlingame	Le Baron Hotel	1970	
Clearmont	Harvey Mudd College		
Death Valley Junction	Amargosa Hotel	1956	
Death Valley			
National Park	Furnace Creek Ranch		
El Segundo	Scientific Data System food service	1967	
Goleta	General Motors Cafeteria		
Hollywood	restaurant		
Huntington Beach	McDonnell Douglas food service		
Kings Canyon			
National Park	Food service		
Laguna Beach	Victor Hugo Inn		
Loma Linda	Harvey House Restaurant	1966	
Los Angeles	Hollywood Restaurant	1939	
Los Angeles	Music Center	1964	
Los Angeles	Airport-Marina Hotel	1969	
Napa	Silverado Properties	1968	
Newhall	Ranch House Restaurant		
Palm Springs	Palm Springs Municipal Airport	1968	
San Juan Capistrano	El Adobe Restaurant	1957	
Santa Barbara	General Motors Defense Systems	1961	
Saugus	Valencia Club House		
Sequoia National Park	Food service	1966?	
Tejon	Tejon Ranch House Restaurant		
Valencia	Ranch House & Club House		
Hawaii			
Waikiki	Liberty House		
Illinois			
Chicago	Kungsholm Restaurant		
Chicago	Playboy Building "Rabbiteria"	1968	
Chicago	Straus Building; Maillard Restaurant		

CITY	HOTEL/RESTAURANT	OPEN	CLOSE
Chicago	Harvey House Restaurant		
Chicago	Bowl & Bottle Restaurant		
Chicago	Harlequin Room		
Chicago	Riverside Plaza Harvey House	1962	
Chicago	Riverside Plaza Coin Café		
Chicago	Field Building Drug Store		
Chicago	Harvey House Grill		
Chicago	Continental Co. Building Cafeteria, Continental Club		
Chicago	Century of Progress Exposition, Toy Town Tavern	1933	
Chicago	Midway Airport restaurants		
Chicago	Strauss Building restaurant		
Harvey	Admiral Corporation food service		
Hinsdale	Old Spinning Wheel		
Illinois Tollway	Oasis restaurants		
Petersburg	New Salem Lodge		
Kansas			
Topeka	Harvey House Restaurant	1966	
Michigan			
Flint	American Way (Unit)	1960s	
Grand Rapids	Kent County Airport Restaurant		
Lansing	Airport restaurant		
Missouri			
Hazelwood	Harvey House Restaurant	1966	
Kansas City	Blue Rooster Restaurant		
Kansas City	First National Bank of Kansas City		
Kansas City	Blue Ridge Cafeteria	1957	
St. Louis	International Fur Exchange Building Restaurant	1964	
St. Louis	St. Louis Bank Building		
St. Louis	Job Corps Center food service	1966	

CITY	HOTEL/RESTAURANT	OPEN	CLOSE
Nebraska			
Lincoln Airport	The Compass Room	1969	
New Mexico			
Albuquerque Airport	Kiva Room, commissary		
Albuquerque	Albuquerque City Club	1965	
Albuquerque	Job Corps food service		
Albuquerque	Trans World Airlines in-flight		
Albuquerque	Frontier Airlines in-flight		
Albuquerque	Monarch Airlines in-flight		
Albuquerque	Continental Airlines in-flight		
Albuquerque	Trans-Texas Airlines in-flight		
Nevada			
Las Vegas Airport	The Ready Room	1969	
Ohio			
Lakewood	Lake Shore Hotel	1960s	
Shaker Heights	Gruber's Restaurant		
Springfield	Shawnee Hotel	1965	
Tennessee			
Memphis	First National Bank of Memphis		
Washington			
Mt. Rainier			
National Park	Food service		
Wisconsin			
Beloit	Harvey House Restaurant	1965	
Wisconsin Dells	Crandell Hotel	1954	
West Virginia			
Charleston	Kanahwa Hotel	1960s	

INDEX

Seafood

FISH

Finnan Haddie   68
Fruite de Mer   72
Mahi-mahi   73
Pompano   71
Salmon, Marinated   69
Salmon Steaks   69

LOBSTER

Lobster Americaine   70

SHRIMP

Shrimp Maciel   70
Shrimp Marguez   68

Soups

Albondigas   18
Bean, Navy   20
Cheese   21
Corn Chowder   19
Currant   20
Posole   18
Vichyssoise   19

Veal

Bourguignonne   51
Cutlet   49
Scallopini, Marsala   49
Scallopini, Piccata   50

Vegetables

Asparagus   93
Bell Pepper, Stuffed   98
Cauliflower, Greens   91
Cauliflower Polonaise   96
Chiles Rellenos   92
Corn   91
Eggplant   96
Frijoles (Beans)   94
Greens   93
Mushrooms, Sauté   94
Mushrooms, Stuffed   92
Onions, Stuffed   95
Potato Soufflé   95
Potatoes, Duchess   98
Potatoes Goufrette   62
Sweet Potatoes   94
Squash   97
Tomatoes, Baked   90
Tomatoes Baked   97
Zucchini, Stuffed   90

The Harvey House Cookbook is the authors' second collaboration; their first coauthored book was *Splendor Sailed the Sound*.

George H. Foster has researched and written extensively on railroading and other maritime subjects. His other previous books include *Steel Rails to the Sunrise*, a history of the Long Island Rail Road, and *Steam in the '60s*, a story of locomotive survival (both with Ron Ziel). He lives with his wife, Helen, in Tucson, Arizona, where he is a marketing consultant and publisher.

Peter C. Weiglin has had a lifelong fascination with railroads. His varied career has included management and consulting work in the U.S. public transportation industry. Besides his previous book coauthored with George Foster, he has published numerous articles on transportation and related subjects. Currently he divides his time between radio and TV production, university teaching, and a marketing and management consulting practice. He and his wife, Jeanne, live in San Mateo, California.